Happy Leap Year!

Leap   Leverage   Dream   Dare

24 • 7 • 366

Dr. Bill Quain

Happy Leap Year

Bill Quain, Ph.D.

Published by Wales Publishing Company
Ocean City, New Jersey

Wales Publishing Company is exclusively owned and operated by Bill Quain

www.quain.com

Cover design and page layout by Parry Design Studio, Inc. - www.parrydesign.com

Printed in the United States of America

First printing - January 2011

Acknowledgements

This book, like all of my pursuits, was a team effort. I would like to particularly acknowledge the efforts of the following Happy Leap Year team members:

Michael Roden—When Michael came to stay with us for about five weeks, I had my doubts about such a long visit. However, when he helped me develop the idea for this book, and then offered to edit it for me, the time flew by. Michael was tireless with his help, even working on the book from the United Kingdom, where he now lives.

Katherine Glover—Katherine knows my market, and she gave generously of her time to help make this book powerful, readable and just plain fun! If you are reading this book, it is probably because Katherine created the distribution channel that reached you.

Jeanne, Amanda and Kathleen Quain—My wife and daughters never cease to amaze me. They are always patient as I try out new ideas, jokes, stories and examples. They sent me back to the drawing board more than once, but were always willing to listen and read.

Jack and Elizabeth Parry—The best thing about knowing Jack and Elizabeth is that I do not need to know anything else! They always do a fantastic job with the book's layout, and with the cover design.

The Gang at Fast Pencil—FP's great writing technology makes it a snap to work with my editors and collaborators. Thanks FP!

Dedication

This book is dedicated to Brother Luke, the coach who taught me to Pole Vault, and to all the members of the LaSalle High School Track Team, past and present.

Table of Contents

Introduction
A Gift For You and Me 1

Chapter One
What Makes a Leap Year So Uncommonly Special? 7

Chapter Two
Confessions of a Leaper 15

Chapter Three
Why Do You Need A Leap Year—Now? 23

Chapter Four
When Should You Shout "Happy Leap Year?" 33

Chapter Five
Before You Leap, Know Where You Want To Land 45

Chapter Six
Are You Worth It? 59

Chapter Seven
How To Develop Leaping Leverage 69

Chapter Eight
Do You Own Your Life or Are You Just Renting? 77

Chapter Nine
**Would You Rather Own Half A Watermelon,
or A Whole Grape?** 89

Chapter Ten
Can The Common Man Create An Uncommon Year? 99

Chapter Eleven
Why Doesn't Everyone Have A Happy Leap Year? 107

Chapter Twelve
Where Will You Be in a Leap Year? 119

Introduction

A Gift for You and Me

Did you ever give someone a gift that you created yourself? Perhaps it was a home-cooked meal, or a knitted sweater, or maybe even something you built, like a piece of furniture. Giving someone a gift like that is a great feeling. You know you did something special. You gave them a gift that they couldn't get anywhere else.

And, when you give a personal gift like that, you get a special gift in return.

Folks, that is how I feel about my latest book, *Happy Leap Year*. It is my personal gift to you. I wrote it for you. This book will help you make a brand-new start on the next Leap Year of your life. And, because I know you are out there, changing your life in positive ways, you help to make my Leap Year special as well.

So, we have started a Leap Year's tradition. You get something, and I get something. Sharing, helping each other grow, and celebrating a special year is a fantastic gift for each of us.

Why I Love Leap Year

I can sum up my feelings about Leap Year in one word—fun! There is just something special about them. Before I started writing this book, I had no idea why we even have Leap Years. (You will soon learn the scientific reasons for it.) Like most people, I just accepted them as a quirky part of our calendar.

I received a great initiation into the fun aspects of Leap Year soon after graduating from college. I had just finished my service year in VISTA (a domestic version of the Peace Corps) and joined my college friends John Williams and Paul Evans, working at a winery in California. John was the winemaker at Stag's Leap Winery, where Paul and I did odd jobs. We lived in a falling-down farmhouse nearby. The owner of the farmhouse was an emergency-room physician who gave us a free place to stay if we helped him rebuild the house.

When we opened up some of the old rooms at the farmhouse, we came across the accounting books for the farm. It seems that the old farmer used to raise frogs to sell to the restaurants in San Francisco. We called the place "The Frog Farm." A few years later, when John opened his own winery, he combined Stag's Leap with the Frog Farm to create his now-famous label Frog's Leap.

Every four years, John Williams puts on a terrific LEAP party on February 29th. I would like to tell you that showing a copy of this book will get you an invitation to the next LEAP party at Frog's Leap but sadly, you must either be a member of the wine business, or have been a roommate of the owner!

I always associated Leap Year with John's incredible sense of humor. He makes business fun, and he is a dream-building business man who always has a smile. So for me, Leap Years mean a good time, good friends, and good business. After you read this book, I hope it will mean the same to you.

Leap Year Is Not A Calendar Event

One of the most important concepts you need to know before reading this book is that your next Leap Year is not a matter of the calendar, it is a matter of your motivation to succeed. You can start your Leap Year at any time. You will read that my first big Leap Year began on July 7, 1993, at 2:30 in the afternoon. Yours could start today, or tomorrow. It may have even started before this.

When you celebrate the principles of Leap Year, you can free yourself from fear, procrastination, out-dated thinking, and even from negative people. If you do it right, it is like every day was February 29—a free day to use as you please. Now, imagine having a free day every day of your life. How would you use it? What would you accomplish that you aren't getting done now?

What About Leap, Leverage, Dream and Dare?

In the subtitle of this book, I give you four keywords you need to embrace in order to take full advantage of Leap Year. They are Leap, Leverage, Dream and Dare. Here is a brief glimpse into the meaning of these words. You will learn much more about them as you read this book.

Leap—You aren't just going to celebrate Leap Year; you will become a Leaper. Learn to jump over obstacles instead of climbing the ladder step-by-step.

Leverage—This is one of the most critical issues that separate most people from well-deserved success. You will learn how I used leverage to out-jump the world record holder in 1967, and how you can Leverage your way to wealth, happiness and success.

Dream—Without a strong, compelling dream, you will never overcome the obstacles to your success. You will still have fear, but you will no longer fear rejection or defeat. Instead, you will fear the loss of your dreams—and this will drive you to succeed.

Dare—What is the most important ingredient for success? Dare to be different. When you Leap, Leverage and Dream, you are different. The question is, "Can you sustain the daring attitude and turn it into actions?"

Start By Wishing Everyone A Happy Leap Year!

As I put the finishing touches on this book, it is January 3, 2011. I have been answering my phone with a new greeting, "Happy Leap Year!" Several people said to me, "I didn't realize this was a Leap Year." My reply has been, "It is for me."

Folks, here is my advice. Make "Happy Leap Year" your standard greeting. To succeed today, you need to be different. You want people to see you as different. Start acting differently by changing the way you greet the world. It doesn't have to be, "Happy Leap Year" but it may need to be something you aren't saying (or doing) today.

When you begin to Leap and Leverage, you will attract a new crowd of friends and associates. Be cheerful, be fun and be committed to spreading the Leap Year message to others. Build a big dream, and Dare to achieve it. Don't ever stop.

You can do it. You have plenty of time. After all, you are Leaping, Leveraging, Dreaming and Daring 24/7/366.

Happy Leap Year to all my readers.

Thank you for the gift.

Chapter One

What Makes a Leap Year So Uncommonly Special?

> *"Leap...and the net will appear"*
>
> John Burroughs, Essayist

*L*eap Years have a fascinating history; they are unique. Through the years, many countries have given them special treatment. In this book, you are going to learn how to make every year a Leap Year, and how to start a Leap Year whenever you need it.

In this chapter, I am going to give you some interesting facts about Leap Years, and describe some myths and rumors that make Leap Years so much fun. However, I am also going to give you the background you need to understand why making this year a Leap Year can also change your life for the better—permanently.

The most important thing you can take away from this chapter is that Leap Years are uncommon. They are uncommon because we call the other three years "Common Years". So, the question is, would you rather have a Leap Year this year, or a common year? Of course, you have already had many common years in your life. We hope to help you make a change. A year from now, would you like to look back on a common year or an uncommon year—a Leap Year? Would you like to build wealth, health and happiness 24/7/366?

Leap Year—a History of the Magic

The concept of a leap year has been around for a long time. Here's the problem. Our modern calendar has 365 days. This is close but not quite accurate. As it turns out, a year is actually 365 *and a quarter days*. This is why, every four years, we require an extra day in our calendar.

To fix this problem Julius Caesar, in 45BC, declared a new Calendar called the Julian calendar that would serve as the legal calendar for the Empire. This calendar included adding one day every four years, known as a "Leap Day," and the year would be known as the "Leap Year." This calendar survived intact for more than fifteen hundred years. For technical reasons, in 1582, Pope Gregory declared a new calendar, called, naturally enough, the Gregorian Calendar.

Over the next two hundred years the rest of the world finally adopted the Gregorian Calendar, but it came by fits and starts. Sweden adopted the new version in 1700, but unaccountably forgot to apply the Leap Day in 1704 and 1708. Thus, in 1712, Sweden achieved immortality by, for the only time in recorded history, announcing a "double leap day" and having the first, and only, February 30th.

In an even more bizarre Leap Year related event, in 1751, the British and their colonies (including America) passed the British Calendar Act, adopting the Gregorian calendar. But, to reconcile their calendar with the new one, they actually had to skip eleven days that year (the things some people will do to achieve a Leap!) The result was that the 2nd of September fell on a Wednesday and the following day, Thursday, became September 14th. There is an ongoing story that there were riots over this move, with people wanting back their "eleven days of existence", but this appears to be an urban myth inspired by a painting of the time.

Most of the rest of the world caught up, but Russia didn't convert until after the revolution in 1918, and Greece not until 1923. There is still a persistent belief in Greece that it is unlucky to marry in a leap year, and many couples postpone weddings because of this belief. In fact, many Orthodox churches still operate on the old Julian calendar—the differences are now approaching two weeks. In large parts of Asia, days and weeks are computed by a "Lunar Calendar" and every two or three years they must insert a "Leap Month". So, you see, you can "Leap" by the Year, the Month and the Day and, in fact, even by the Second. Every eighteen months, the Calendar is adjusted one second, due to influence of weather, and the gravitational effect of the other planets in the Solar System.

Then, of course, there is the wonderful tradition, supposedly beginning with a plea from St. Bridgid to St. Patrick, asking that women be allowed to propose to men during a Leap Year. This tradition made its way down to the Leap Day only, but several countries passed legislation concerning this day, with fines imposed on the men who refused the proposal. Will a similar fine be imposed on you, if you refuse to accept my proposal to turn your next 366 days into a happy Leap Year?

Thus we can see that Leap Year has both a scientific basis and an emotional background that makes it rich indeed. Possibly the idea may make you rich too.

Happy Uncommon Year

Okay, you now know that Leap Years are different, and that common customs and rules do not apply. It is time for you to read on—and get the knowledge and motivation you need to have an uncommon year. It isn't hard to do. All you need is a little imagination, and a strong dream.

In the following chapters, you will get a guided tour for a Happy Leap Year. We want you to jump into a new life—one full of promise, wealth and fun.

You need an uncommon year because success, *real success*, is also uncommon. How many really successful people do you know? Which is more common in your experience; common people, or uncommon people? In the next chapter, you will read about the first Happy Leap Year Day of my life. I can tell you this; the people I knew before I began to change my life were all commoners—just like me. We worked hard, had jobs, did what we were supposed to do, and lived quite common lives.

Unfortunately, I didn't want to settle for "common" or "ordinary." I wanted something special. I wanted something uncommon.

It never occurred to me that I needed to come up with an uncommon plan for my life. In fact, I needed an uncommon year. I needed a Leap Year.

When St. Brigid asked St. Patrick to give women permission to ask men to marry them, she was doing something extraordinary. If you want to live a wonderful life, free from financial stress, with lots of time to enjoy your family, can you see how that is just as daring?

Leap Years are uncommonly good; living the life of a Leaper is also uncommonly good. Put them both together, and Leap.

The Common New Year Isn't So Common Either

I couldn't write a chapter about Leap Year without taking a look at all New Year's traditions—common or Leap. We take so many things for granted that it is essential to point out that many of our traditions are quite arbitrary. For example, did you know that celebrating New Year's Day on January 1 is a relatively recent tradition? Is that a surprise to you? It shocked me! I just *assumed* that January 1 was always the first day of the New Year. But, that just goes to show you that we can't get trapped by things we believe to be permanent. We need to adjust our thinking in order to be successful.

The earliest known New Year's celebrations came from the ancient Babylonians. Their New Year began on March 21, the Vernal Equinox. In fact, many cultures celebrated the New Year during the end of winter and the beginning of spring. Spring is a time of rebirth, so it makes sense to start the New Year during the planting and thawing time of the year.

Some cultures celebrated the New Year in the fall, others during the winter solstice. Each culture had its own views on the subject.

The Big Reason January 1 Wasn't New Year's Day

The biggest reason that January 1 was not the first day of the year is because January did not exist as a month until the Roman times. The original Roman calendar had only ten months. (September comes from the word for "seven" so it makes sense that it should have been the seventh month in the original calendar.) January 1 was the start of the Roman Civil calendar, much like a fiscal calendar in today's terms.

About 1,000 years ago the Church banned New Year's celebrations, because they were too much like pagan feasts. It wasn't until the sixteenth century that Pope Gregory reinstated the traditions of a New Year's festivity.

Can you see what implications this has for you? You don't need to start your Leap Year on January 1. You can do like almost everyone else has done over the centuries and start it whenever you like! Break with tradition, and break into a New Year with positive, passionate enthusiasm.

Other Traditions to Use – Or Lose

Songs—"Auld Lang Syne" is sung in every English-speaking country on New Year's Eve. The title is an old Scottish phrase that means "the good old days." While the tune is much older, the modern version of the lyrics was written by Robert Burns in the early 1700s. If you want to have something interesting to talk about, learn the lyrics to the song. There are a number of stanzas.

Food—Different cultures have different foods for the New Year. My wife is of Norwegian descent (Her mother is first-generation American.) We always eat pickled herring for good luck on January 1. Other traditional foods are pork (prosperity), cabbage (the leaves are a reminder of paper money) and rice (yes, the same food they throw at brides).

The First Visitor—The first visitor to your home can auger good luck or bad. Traditionally, if the first visitor is a tall, dark-haired man, it is good luck. Now, I don't know what this means for you, since the author of this book is neither tall nor dark-haired, but we can just hope for the best.

The point is this; you can create your own New Year's celebrations and traditions any time you want, for any day you want. My wife and I have our Happy Leap Year traditions because of our experience with July 7 (see next chapter). You need to mark the day you change your life, and you can do it anytime, and in any way, that you desire. After all, everyone else did.

New Year's Resolutions

Of course, nothing says "Happy New Year" or "Happy Leap Year" like a New Year's Resolution. (You will find a place to make some Resolutions at the end of each chapter in this book.)

Resolutions, like the times, have changed over the centuries. In ancient Babylon the most common resolution, according to one website I found, was "To return borrowed farm equipment." I polled many of my friends this year, and NONE of them are resolving to return farm equipment. However, if you have borrowed a tractor or a harvester, just put on your Babylonian finery and get it back to the rightful owner ASAP.

As I did some research for this book, I thought that "losing weight" was probably going to be the most popular Resolution in the United States. A website I found confirmed that, and provided their list of the top ten Resolutions.

Here they are:

1. Lose Weight
2. Manage Debt/Save Money
3. Get a Better Job
4. Spend More Time with Family
5. Quit Smoking
6. Eat Right/Get Fit
7. Get a Better Education
8. Reduce Stress
9. Go Greener
10. Volunteer to Help Others

For those of you who are planning to lose weight in the next year, I have some good news. Actually, the good news is from Jay Leno. Here is his take on the situation:

"Now there are more overweight people in America than average-weight people so overweight people are now average. This means you've met your New Year's resolution."

In the space below, write your Leap Year Resolution to be different this year. Why will this year be an uncommon year?

We'll break through the mental barriers to be brand new Platinums in FY12

What will you do differently?

Speak our goals everyday; think & act positive all the time

Chapter Two

Confessions of a Leaper

> *"Oh the wild joys of living!*
> *The leaping from rock to rock ...*
> *the cool silver shock of the plunge*
> *in a pool's living waters."*
>
> Robert Browning

I am a Leaper. I want to help you become a Leaper too. Leapers jump over obstacles, and save themselves time and money by going right to the target—their goals. Leapers are not held back by the conventional wisdom that says that you have to work hard at a job to get ahead. Leapers understand that the best way to achieve great goals is to use "Leverage," make bold moves, and take risk. But, Leapers also know that it is possible to risk things other than money and time. Leapers risk their reputations perhaps, but never their principles. They understand that Leaping may make them unpopular in some circumstances, but they also understand that the people who dislike Leapers are the same people who will never know the taste of freedom and satisfaction. Finally, Leapers understand that there are other Leapers out there and that, by Leaping, they will find them.

So again, I confess, I am a Leaper. I am proud to be one. It has changed my life in so many wonderful ways. Yes, some of my friends have a difficult time understanding my outlook on life. Yes, some people dislike me because I became a Leaper. But the rewards—in money, time, friendship and satisfaction—are outstanding. As a Leaper, I learned the one great secret of Leapers. I learned to *leverage* my effort so that my Leap was more than just a jump. My Leaps became giant shifts in my fortune.

As a Leaper, I learned to enjoy a very special time—Leap Year, and, as a Leaper, I learned that Leap Year's Day can start anytime.

I confess; I am a Leaper, and I love it. I would love you to become a Leaper too.

My Happy Leap Year Story

My first Happy Leap Year Day occurred on July 7, 1993. To be precise, my day actually started at 2:30 p.m. (This was my midnight, when the ball dropped and my Happy Leap Year began.)

At that time, we were living in Orlando, Florida, and I was a college professor, author and professional speaker. We liked our home in Orlando, but it was in the middle of the state, and we wanted to live on the water. Whenever we were around the ocean, we would say to ourselves, "We have to move to the water, and live there, with a boat and a nice house."

On that particular Happy Leap Year Day (July 7, 1993), I had just given a talk to a group in Fort Lauderdale, and we were sitting at a waterside table eating a late lunch. It was a hot day, and the ice in our glasses was causing the condensation to form on the outside of the glass. Jeanne was pregnant with our second daughter, Kathleen, and our older daughter was asleep in a stroller beside the table.

Suddenly a shadow fell across the table, and I looked up to see a large yacht going by, with happy people celebrating on the stern deck. They were having a wonderful time (I wonder if it was a Happy Leap Year Day for them.)

I remember this day like it was yesterday, not almost 18 years ago. I turned to Jeanne and said, "We need to change our lives. We need to do something different, and move to the water and get a big boat." Jeanne agreed, and we decided to change our lives on July 7, 1993, at 2:30 in the afternoon. It was one minute after midnight on our first Happy Leap Year Day!

What Did We Do?

In order to achieve our dreams and move to the water, Jeanne and I knew we had to make some big changes in our lives. We knew the old rules we were living by would not accomplish what we wanted. For us, the answer was simple—establish a business that had no ceiling on the amount of money we could make, and then conduct that business in such a way that we were able to leverage our time and money so that we could enjoy our new life.

We needed to use a new set of practices, principles and procedures. We needed a Leap Year Mentality to overcome the normal barriers that would prevent a college professor from enjoying a life style on the water, with a big boat and a nice house.

You see folks, that was the problem. I was a college professor, making some decent money, and enjoying a comfortable lifestyle. But, I knew one thing when I saw that yacht go by, with those happy people on it. I knew that none of them were making their lifestyle dreams come true by being a college professor. I knew a LOT of college professors, and none of them had a yacht like that.

How about you? Do people who do what you do have yachts? Do they live on the water and have plenty of time to spend with their families? Do the people who do what you do have all the things and benefits you dream of having? Throughout this book, you will read my words about "working for someone else's dream." I will talk about the problems of "trading your time for money on a job." Please don't think that I am making fun of people with jobs, or saying that having a job is a bad thing. I am simply saying that, on July 7, 1993, at 2:30 in the afternoon, I came to the sudden realization that my job was not going to give me what I wanted. I came to the dead-serious conclusion that I had to make some changes.

Our Leap of Faith

Instead of looking at the people who were doing the same things we were doing (working on a job) and thinking, "If I can only work harder and longer than they do, I will get ahead," we looked around to find people who were living like we wanted to live, and found that entrepreneurs had what we wanted. They had no ceiling on the amount of money they could make and, if they were in the right kind of business, they also could leverage their time so they could enjoy life. We started learning the rules of a new kind of wealth-creation model, and soon were well on our way to living on the water.

It actually took about five years, but we did it. We had a beautiful home on the water, with our 30-foot boat in the back yard. We fished in some major tournaments, and my oldest daughter qualified for the World Championships twice. My younger daughter finished second in the Miami tournament as well.

How did we achieve our dreams? We took a Leap of Faith and tried something different. We knew that we might fail. We created a wealth-generating business in our spare time, while I kept my job as a college professor. Believe me, we worked hard! And for me especially, it required some massive shifts in my thinking. After all, I was brought up to think that a great education would lead to financial security. That may have been true at one time. I did have some great security, but what I didn't have was a house on the water with a boat at the dock in my backyard. So we worked like crazy people for those five years and, in the end, we had a different lifestyle. We made it, and it felt great.

We often look back on that exact moment, and we know it changed our lives forever.

When Is YOUR Happy Leap Year Day?

Folks, here is something to consider. You can start your Happy Leap Year ANY TIME YOU WANT. You can even restart it. It is totally up to you. No one will say, "This isn't New Year's Day". Maybe you will never have a Happy Leap Year Day when a huge yacht goes by and stirs up so much anxiety and longing that you have to change. I hope you have some sort of day like that. But, even without it, you can decide that ANY DAY is the first day of your Happy Leap Year. What will it take to "trigger" the desire to make enough changes so that you can begin Leaping into a new life? When will you finally say, "Okay, this is it? I am going to do whatever it takes to get what I want—and deserve."

Leap-Think

To be a Leaper, you need to develop Leap-Think. Leap-Thinking means that you decide on the rewards first, then open your mind completely to new ways of acting, learning and believing. A Leap-Thinker is always concerned about the outcome, not the process. When most people think about their lives, they see a linear progression from school to a job, to a promotion, to a raise, to more responsibility, to more stuff. They think in a straight line and, because they do, they see obstacles they have to overcome. For example, when ordinary people think about buying a bigger home, they see the obstacle of making money. They know they have to work harder on their job so they can get a raise, and get a promotion. Of course, the promotion means they are working longer hours, and taking work home with them. They don't care, because this is how they see themselves overcoming the "I need more money in order to buy a house" problem.

Leapers are geometric thinkers, not linear thinkers. They see the end-result, then say, "How can I get there the fastest, easiest and most interesting way?" Instead of taking the next, logical step (as defined by their boss) they think, "What have other Leapers done to overcome this problem? How can I apply the lessons I learned from them, rather than simply climbing up the ladder rung after rung?"

Now, at first, this may seem like Leapers are trying to cheat the system. It may seem like they are trying to get something for nothing. But this is typical linear thinking. A linear thinking person cannot see other possibilities. They only know what they are told by the person right in front.

The Key to Leaping

The key to Leaping is to spend more time moving forward than moving up. Leapers know that the big goals, the big rewards, are not "up the next rung of the ladder." The big goals are ahead. They can only be reached by massive changes in thinking and actions.

In this book you will learn some incredible things that will help you make permanent shifts in your family's fortunes. I know you can do it because we did it, and we are just ordinary people. And, it wasn't as if we didn't have challenges and set-backs along the way.

When you have a minute, read my bio in the back of this book. I am legally blind, and can't drive a car. If that isn't a challenge, I don't know what is! When I decided to change my life, on July 7, 1993, at 2:30 in the afternoon, I had to determine a way to create wealth *despite the fact that I could not read printed material, drive a car or travel by myself.*

For me, Leaping really wasn't just a choice I made. It was an absolute *necessity* if I wanted to have more than most handicapped people have. I didn't just need to overcome the obstacles of being paid a paycheck as a state employee; I had to overcome the obstacle of being a handicapped state employee.

I had to leap over both those hurdles before I could start enjoying my lifestyle. Handicapped people don't usually own boats, and college professors who work for the state don't usually live on the water. I was Leaping from *deep inside a hole!*

Are you leaping from a hole as well? It really doesn't matter. Wherever you are right now is where you are right now. If you are really hurting, the leap will be higher; if you are in pretty good shape, then you may be able to make a shorter leap. But I can promise you this. If you do not do something FAST, you are not going to do anything at all. It doesn't matter how long it takes you, it only matters if you *begin*.

By the end of this book, you should be ready to make a confession that you are a Leaper too.

One of the most important things for you to realize is that there will be a "sign" or "signal" that will trigger your need to declare a Happy Leap Year. However, you must be ready to recognize it.

In the space below, I would like you to answer the following questions with some short statements.

1. Are you prepared to watch for a sign or signal that you must make changes?

   Yes

2. Have you already seen your signal, and if so, what was it?

   Seeing the huge crowds at ~~this~~ the US Open — I need to be here

3. Will you resolve to take action, no matter how difficult it will be for you?

   Yes, I'm doing it every day

Chapter Three

Why Do You Need A Leap Year—NOW?

> *"Half the failures in life arise from pulling in one's horse as he is leaping."*
>
> August Hare, Author

*T*he world is changing at such a crazy, reckless pace that you need to do something special—RIGHT NOW. The next 366 days are critical for your family's future. If you wait, if you hesitate and if you cling to your old hopes for prosperity, you will be lost.

I have been writing books about wealth building since 1993. That year, I warned people about the dangers of depending on a job for financial security. In those days, many companies were going bankrupt, and hundreds of thousands of people were losing their jobs. In that first wealth-building book, I showed ordinary men and women how to change their thinking, and how to adjust to a rapidly changing world.

Well, we *thought* it was rapidly changing. As it turns out, we had no idea back then of just how RAPID, RAPID could be! In those days, businesses were just learning the importance of laying off workers as productivity increased. And, as the financial system went into crisis, in a bad recession, many people lost their jobs, and lost the value of many investments. For example, retirement savings were decimated as stocks plunged and as the value of real estate fell.

That was in the early 1990s. At that time, we were just learning that the old adage, "Get a good education, and get a good job, and things will be great" no longer applied to modern business practices. Before that, we all looked at corporations as the great benefactors that would take care of us for a lifetime. It was an "arranged marriage." When you took a job, you kept it until you either got fired or retired. If you lasted until retirement, and most people did, you got a good pension. Between your pension and your Social Security check, you could do all right.

But, we learned a different lesson in the 1990s, and I wrote about it.

The More Things Change...

There is an old saying, "The more things change, the more they stay the same." Well, in some sense, that is true. We just came through a terrible recession—one that was much worse than the 1988—1992 upset. Yet, many of the problems we saw then—high unemployment, huge numbers of jobless people, a decline in the value of homes and other investments, and a general despair about the future—are the exact same indicators we see today. From that perspective, it is true; the more things change, the more they stay the same.

However, I would like to propose a new saying. It is, "The more things change, the faster they start to change." In our hectic, revolutionary world of ever-changing technology and high finance, things are changing so quickly that it is almost impossible to keep up with them.

For example, today I did three things that I would not have dreamed of just two years ago. I posted a comment on two blogs, made a new post on my own blog, updated my Facebook profile, and made a video and posted it to my website. Now, I need to remind you, I am 58 years old and, as many of you know, I am legally blind! How is it possible for me, a handicapped older guy, to do those things?

You see folks, things have changed so quickly that no one even thinks it is unusual for me to do this. It wouldn't have happened just twenty-four months ago!

When I published my first wealth-building book back in the early 1990s, it took forever to edit it and get it printed. In addition, we had to send out faxes, and wait for checks to arrive to collect money. Today, I simply open an account on PayPal, set up a website, and I am in business. The name of the game today is speed. As one of my graduate assistants used to say, "Come on, come on, we haven't got all second."

Unlike 1993, when we say "Things are changing so quickly" today, we are right! But, think of this; if things have speeded up in the last 18 years, how fast will they be going 18 years from now? In fact, how fast will they be changing *this year*?

Twin Problems

Here is the situation. Once again the economy has collapsed, and the ordinary men and women got hurt. We are the ones who have to pay mortgages with less money—or no money. We are the ones who lost our retirement savings in the stock market, and we are the ones who have homes that are worth less today than when we bought them. Our ability to retire, or even to live decently, has been greatly eroded by forces beyond our control. Yet this is NOT the first time this has happened, nor will it be the last.

On the other hand, we are faced with a world that is vastly different than it was twenty years ago, and even different than it was two years ago. The world's economies are merging. Communications advances make it possible to stay in touch every second of every day. We are so bombarded with messages that we keep missing the one message that would help us solve our current problems, and keep them from happening to us again.

Why is it that we all know that the economy is not "fixed," and yet we continue to look for the same solutions? Why is it that we are getting a continuous news feed about lay-offs, unemployment, bankruptcies and other financial problems, yet we still try to solve our problems by going back to work for the same people who ruined the economy, and our financial security, just a few years ago?

Folks, you need something different, and you need it fast. You have two problems, and you need to learn from the one, and grow with the other. You need to understand that working on a job is NEVER going to solve your financial problems, and you need to adjust your thinking so that you can respond and adapt to the new realities of change and disruption.

Did This Work?

Before you read this next session, let me apologize to you if you are not from the United States, or if you are not familiar with the things we just went through. I do not know what other countries did, but I assume that they are somewhat similar.

In the United States, we spent *billions* on a stimulus bill to prevent unemployment from going over 8%. Did this work?

We gave more *billions* to banks so they would not go out of business, and so they would lend money to us when we needed it for our businesses. Did this work?

We threw out one political party, brought in another, then threw them out and brought back in the first party—all in an effort to gain some financial control and to rebuild our economy and create jobs. Did this work?

We attempted to regulate Wall Street investors so they would not act so recklessly again. Did this work?

We urged our legislators to change government policies that gave loans to people who could not possibly afford them. Did this work?

We watched countries like Ireland and Greece go into virtual bankruptcy and we, as citizens, learned our lessons. We hoped our government would learn them, too. Did this work?

Finally, we learned that our government did NOT learn the lessons we did during the last recession. We all learned to cut back on our spending, and to live within our means. We wrote letters to our legislators, and protested in the capital. Did this work?

Where Are We Heading?

The U.S. isn't the only country with these problems; we are just the *largest* country with these problems. Throughout the world the financial system, and the people who work in it, are in danger of another calamity, perhaps worse than the one we just went through. Yet, while many of us learned valuable lessons and cut back on our lifestyle choices, how many of us have made the *mandatory* adjustments in our thinking to make sure that we can *personally* avoid the dangers that are mounting around us? It is quite easy to imagine that the unsolved problems—either from our government, our financial institutions, or ourselves—will almost certainly lead to challenges in the very near future.

But, how do we ask for help? Do we say, "Show me how to think differently so that I can develop a new course of action?" No, we say "Help create more jobs." It doesn't make sense.

On top of it all is the unbelievable speed that is warping the senses and making every decision a critical one. Trends that took years to develop now happen in months, or even weeks, as information explodes and our ability to learn about new products and services go through the roof.

Is There Hope?

Yes, there is reason to hope. You see folks, even in this recent downturn, some companies are actually booming. That is the nature of business. Even in the worst of times, the people who see the trends, and who have prepared themselves to do well will survive and thrive. If you understand the past, are aware of the present, and are prepared for the future, you can actually *grow* in a setback. And, of course, if the economy does not have a problem, those same people will do far better than those who cling to the old ways, the old technologies, and the old system of trading time for dollars.

And, it isn't all technology based. The temptation is to say, "Well, companies that brought new technologies are doing well, but everyone else is failing". That just isn't true. Yes, some tech companies like Google, Apple and others, are doing very well. But there are hundreds, no *thousands* of companies that have found a great niche and are working it to great profit.

But, the companies that are doing well do have one thing in common. They are adapting to new circumstances, and new ways of thinking, and, many of the companies are small, single-owner, home-based businesses that have low entry costs, and unlimited potential upside, and, many of the companies are giving the participants a "fraction of the action" as profit-sharing partners.

You will learn more about that in this book but, for now, let's concentrate on you, and what you need to be doing to prepare for the coming changes.

Learn Your Lessons, and Change Quickly

I want you to examine your situation, and make some decisions. Do you depend on a job for your financial security? If you do, you are in trouble. If not now, you will be in trouble shortly. It may not be from this recession, but it will happen.

Have you taken advantage of the endless possibilities and developed a Personal Strategy for Success? You must. It may require a change in thinking, but you must have the ability to quickly and permanently build equity. You cannot build equity on a job. You must have your own business.

Do you believe that someone else is going to solve your upcoming problems? Do you think your government is going to have a safety net in place for you and, even if they do, do you want to fall into it? Do you think that your boss, or the company you work for are thinking about your future and how to protect it? Do you believe they will take care of you when you cannot perform your job anymore, or when they can't afford to keep you?

Folks, there is only one person in the whole world who will care about your future and, of course, it is you. Yes, your spouse and children or your parents also may care, but the responsibility lies directly with you.

Fortunately, you can make the changes necessary. It is not too late, and the circumstances have never been better.

Are You Kidding? What Do You Mean "The Circumstances Have Never Been Better?"

Yes, you read it right. I believe that the circumstances have never been better for individuals like us. This is the perfect time for us. Once again, there are twin reasons.

Firstly, technology and the ability to communicate quickly and inexpensively have never been better, and it is certain to get even easier and cheaper.

Secondly, no one in their right minds would think that doing the same old thing is going to work, so it is actually easier to make changes in your thinking and actions today than it ever was. Also, it is easier to find other people to work with.

In fact, the timing is perfect. Now all you have to do is to take action.

Look Behind You, Then Look Ahead

Folks, look behind you. There is nothing there for you; your bridges are burned; you can't go back.

Now, look to the future. You are going to get there whether you get there prepared, or unprepared. You can only move forward and, guess what, that is a *good* thing, because your best times are yet to come.

In the past, you had common years. In the future, if you decide to embrace it and prepare for it, you can have Leap Years. I have chosen to Leap. How about You?

I am making a Resolution to look through this book for answers. I know that the past will repeat itself. My job is to make sure I do not repeat my old mistakes. With my open mind, I will consider new ideas, and prepare for new outcomes. In the space below, briefly describe what you would like to learn from this book. Resolve to find it, and implement it.

Chapter Four

When Should You Shout "Happy Leap Year?"

> *"We must walk consciously only part-way toward our goal, and then leap in the dark to our success."*
>
> Henry David Thoreau, Philosopher

*I*t isn't going to do you any good to wake up one morning and shout, "Happy Leap Year" and expect your life to change. As I am always fond of saying at my presentations, "If you want to change your life, you have to *change* your life." It is not the act of saying something that creates change; it is the act of actually changing something.

Nonetheless, you do need to pick a date, and you do need to shout "Happy Leap Year" on the day you start to change. It is not only a lot of fun; it is an essential part of taking the Leap.

There are five steps (or stages) that you will go through to take your first Leap, but you only need to experience the first three in order to declare your "Happy Leap Year." The first step, or stage, is to recognize that you have a problem. Once you do this, you can begin to solve the problem. I had that situation on July 7, 1993. When will it happen to you?

Let's look at the Five Stages in some detail, and then start Leaping.

Five Steps to a Leap

In order to declare your Happy Leap Year and start leaping, you must meet five conditions, or go through the "Five Steps to a Leap" process. They are:

1. Recognize that you have a problem

2. Define your dream in specific terms

3. Make a commitment to your dream
   (Now you can shout "Happy Leap Year.")

4. Find people who have already solved the problem, and do what they did

5. Execute your plan, then do it again

Let's talk about each of these stages so that you understand exactly what you need to do. I can't guarantee you that following them will give you everything you want, every time. But I can tell you that if you do not follow these steps, you will never have what you want.

Recognize that you have a problem

For me, the Problem Recognition came all at once, on July 7, 1993. In fact, it hit me **EXACTLY** at 2:30 in the afternoon. For other people, the Problem Recognition stage happens more slowly. But, whether it happens all at once, or over time, here is what happens. At some point, you realize that you are never going to have anything more than you have now—unless you make some changes. That's it; it is very basic. Your mind just seems to understand.

For some people, it is when a boss comes into their office and says one of the following:

- Our profits are down, and we have to lay you off
- You didn't get the raise and the promotion; _____ got it. (Fill in that blank with the name of the person who always gets things like that, even though you deserve it more)
- I am sorry it is your child's birthday, but this meeting is really important
- Etc. etc.

Or, maybe it is when your spouse says:

- I am so tired. When can we stop working so hard?
- We never seem to see each other anymore
- Honey, I know the new baby is only six weeks old, but we need the money
- The _____ (fill in the blank with the name of that pesky family down the street) are going on vacation, and asked us to go along
- Don't you recognize that kid? He is your son. You really need to get more involved (Okay, maybe that one is a little overdone!)

Or, when your child says:

- Can we go to Disney World this year?
- I want to go to college, can we afford it?
- Dad, can you come to my play this time? All the other kids' dads will be there

Or maybe you are a shallow, self-centered person like me, and you will finally see the problem when a big boat goes by you! Maybe for you, it is a car, or a racehorse or a castle in Monte Carlo. Whatever it is, it doesn't matter. Just thank God that it happened!

Many people never have that shock of Problem Recognition. These people never will know the joy of shouting "Happy Leap Year." They just go on and on, doing the same things they always did, and wondering why they just can't seem to get ahead.

I hope you are not one of these people who never get the "shock" of problem recognition. I hope you are one of the lucky ones—like me—who suddenly saw the true state of things, and then Leaped into the unknown and changed their lives forever.

Yes, it can be uncomfortable; yes, it can hurt, but it is the best thing that will ever happen in your life.

Why don't more people have Problem Recognition? The answer is sad. Most of them are so busy putting one foot in front of the other, trying to make a broken system work for them, trying to make their way through the maze by going up one row and down another, that they never see the problem.

Let me repeat; the obstacle for most people is that they don't see the problem. The problem for almost all people is that they are doing something that will never give them what they want. They are in a broken system, and it just will not get any better.

Folks, don't be like most people. Look around you. If you are in the same place that you were a year ago, or if you are worse off than you were a year ago, you need to start a Happy Leap Year program NOW!

Define Your Dream in specific terms

Some people will argue that the dream comes first, and then the Problem Recognition. However, most people's dreams are ill-defined and hazy. They may want something more, but they have never spent the time to really define **EXACTLY** what their dream is. And, in most cases, people don't define their dreams until they have made a decision to go after it. I find that this happens more often after Problem Recognition.

It happened to me on July 7, 1993. I had a good idea that I wanted to live on the water, but, along with my wife Jeanne, we didn't really define the dream until after the shock of our Problem Recognition.

So, let's talk a bit about your dreams. What are they? What do you want? When will you get it? Is there any way to achieve your dreams without making drastic changes to your situation?

There are dozens of books out there about dream building. (I wrote several of them!). I won't spend a lot of time discussing it now, but let me give you a few thoughts:

- **Dream in Stages**—If you have very little right now, if you are barely scraping by, don't say "By this time next year, I will be a multi-millionaire and live in a skyscraper penthouse." Be realistic

- **Don't go Too Small**—On the other hand, don't make your dreams so small and confining that you never even break a sweat when you go after them. Dreams should stretch you, and put you out of your comfort zone. For example, don't set a dream for a new set of golf clubs that cost $600

- **Aim for Lifestyle**—It is just fine to have dreams about material things, like cars and boats. (After all, it was enough to get me moving!) However, the best dreams, the most compelling dreams, are those that involve lifestyle. This means you have money **And the Time** to enjoy it

- **Create Spiritual Dreams**—Wouldn't it be nice to have so much that your only new challenge would be how to give some of it away? Set spiritual dreams that involve helping others. It may be family members or complete strangers

- **Own your dreams**—If you are serious about getting the things you want, you must own the ideas. Commit to them. Make them real by talking about them with important people in your life

- **Leap for Them**—You will never achieve your dreams by continuing to do what you have always done. Make the Leap. Do the work. Achieve your dreams

- **Commit to your Dreams**—When you commit to your dreams, you are making a promise. You promise to do everything in your power to achieve the specific dreams you set. It is like your marriage vows. You declare them "in front of God and this company".

When we decided to pursue our dreams, it changed our lives. This is not to say, "We achieved our dreams, and then our lives changed," but rather, "Our lives changed the minute we committed to our dreams." It is the act of commitment that begins your Leap. When we declared our intentions, and decided that we would do everything in our power to attain our dreams, we became different people. Suddenly, we had the energy and desire to do things that we never did before. And, most importantly, because we were both committed to the dreams, we understood when the other person had to do something extra, like work harder, or spend some time building a business. Our commitment to mutual dreams made us a team, and that team spirit achieved our dreams. It was the commitment.

There is an old story about a chicken and a pig walking down the road, and they spot a sign that reads, "St. Peter's Church; Ham and Egg Breakfast."

The chicken said to the pig, "Shall we go inside and help?" The pig replied, "No way; for you it is a donation, but for me it is a total commitment!"

What about you? Do you have a dream that is so strong that you are willing to make a total commitment to achieve it? Will you sacrifice it all for the dream?

You see, folks, this is where a higher level dream is important. Yes, it is fine to have a dream about a new car or boat; it is fine to have a dream about money, or a cruise or vacation. But the real commitment comes from the real dreams. When you want a *thing,* you are not willing to give up the time and energy necessary to attain it. But, when you want a *lifestyle,* you are *temporarily* giving up some time and money in order to attain a new lifestyle—which is money, and the time to enjoy it.

Commit to your dreams, but make sure your dreams are worth the effort! Think long-term. Do some short-term things if you need to, but go for the lifestyle you deserve. Commit to it and live the dream.

Find people who have already solved your problem, and do what they did. There is very little "new" in this world. If your problem is that you do not have enough time to spend with your kids, then you can certainly find people who had the same problem. If your problem is that your bills are greater than your income, or that your mortgage payment is so high that you can't imagine how you are going to keep the house, then you need to take the same action as other people who have already solved this problem.

The secret is to identify the system that they used. You probably got into the mess you are in by following some kind of system, didn't you? After all, if you are broke, or worried about becoming broke, or unable to afford a vacation, or you are working so hard that you do not have time for anyone else, then you got that way by following a bad system. Or, you might have followed a good system *badly*. Either way, you need to get around different people in your life. You need to find the type of people you want to be, not hang around with the kind of people you already are!

Did you catch that last bit of advice? Part of leaping is to leap to a spot where the real heroes of your life already exist. You need to leap out of the trap of always being around other people just like you. You don't need to dump them. Just stop looking to them for solutions to your problems. Find people who are successful, identify the system they use, and then follow them and the system.

Folks, there is absolutely no reason to do this on your own. Later in this book you will learn about creating equity by building ownership. One of the things that you can own right away is a system. Don't waste your time reinventing the wheel. Just find a system that works, and work that system!

If you have a problem, it is probably because you do not know how to do something different. If you did, you would not have the problem.

Let me give you an example. A mythical couple, John and Susan, have worked hard all their lives. They both work a full week. John is a manager for a publisher, and Susan is a teacher.

After ten years, they have a house, but it has a large mortgage. They have cars, but they also owe the bank for the car loans. They took a nice vacation last year, and they have the credit cards to prove it!

A week ago, John got a notice that his publishing company was laying off people. He was not laid off, but he had to take a pay cut. Still, he is concerned. The publishing industry is not doing well. Will he be the next one to be laid off?

John and Susan got a great big dose of **Problem Recognition!** Their nice, secure lifestyle is threatened. They had not yet begun to save money for their children's college education. They had a vague dream about buying a vacation home in a few years. But, none of that is worrying them right now, because they are wondering if they will be able to pay the mortgage in a few months.

The shock of **Problem Recognition** is stunning! It keeps them awake at night. They decide to do something about it.

John and Susan have just gone through stage 1 **(Problem Recognition)** and they will soon go through stages 2 **(Define their Dream)** and 3 **(Commit to that Dream)**. However, when it comes to stage 4, they are stopped in their tracks. Why is that? The answer is simple—neither of them has the slightest idea of how to make the Leap and achieve their dreams. Susan was always a grade-school teacher. What experience would she have with massive, life-changing business decisions? John works in a business, but his business is in trouble. Would he have any reason to think that working harder for a publisher is a good way to achieve meaningful dreams, no matter how much he commits to them?

The answer, of course, is "absolutely not." Neither of these two people, committed though they are, excited though they might be, have any idea how to build equity and deliver themselves from their financial problems first, then achieve long-term, life-altering, dreams.

One of the major challenges that John and Susan have is that they are hanging around other people who are also in trouble. Do teachers have the answers to these problems? Of course they do not. (I am not making fun of teachers here. But, no one ever said, "I want to be rich like a teacher.")

After work, and on weekends, John hangs around with other people just like himself. What do they talk about? They talk about how difficult it is these days to make ends meet. They discuss the possibility of getting laid off. Do you know what they *do not* talk about? They do not talk about the successful people they know. They do not say, "Let's look at what Pete is doing, and see if we can do the same thing. Pete is doing great. He is always going on vacations and spending time at the country club with his wife and kids."

When Susan has a few minutes in the teachers' lounge at school, does she ask the other teachers, "Has anyone noticed how nicely dressed Veronica is? Let's see if she will share her secrets with us; I would like to make some changes and have what she has." No, instead, like everyone else who works in some kind of business or institution, they talk about how the budget has been cut and they will probably have to pay for the copies themselves!

Am I exaggerating here? I don't think so. I hear it all the time. Instead of talking about successful people, and learning how to make significant changes, most people spend their time with people who are just like them, *complaining or worrying* about the current situation. Look folks, the current situation is *bad; don't* talk about the present. Find a way to make the future better.

You need a new system. You need to follow the example of other people. You need to know that, when you leap, it will be into something good, solid and meaningful.

Folks, if you wanted to make some changes around the house, would you feel comfortable buying some paint and changing the color in your daughter's room? Most of us would be able to do that. After all, it is just a "surface change". But what if you tried to turn the water on and only a small trickle emerged. Would you feel qualified to open the walls and install new pipes? Or would you be willing to tap into a new water source by yourself? Most of us would not want to do those things for the simple reason that we have no idea how to do it! If we did try, we might waste a lot of time and money while we got the experience, and getting the experience might be a very painful thing indeed!

You need to find good people, and follow their system for one simple reason. You do not want to confuse "Do it yourself" with "Do it *by* yourself."

One of the big secrets of Leaping successfully is to leap where others have already gone.

Execute your plan, then do it again—Okay, you discovered you had a problem, and you shouted "Happy Leap Year" to the world. You defined your dream, and made a commitment to it. You identified successful people who have already solved the same problems you faced, and you learned there is a system that works for you. Now, it is time to execute and Leap! Then, you need to execute and Leap again.

Unfortunately, this is **EXACTLY** where most people stop. They get right to the brink, and then they simply stop. Something happens. Maybe a brother-in-law or a "friend" tells them they can't do it. Maybe they become overwhelmed with the need to take action on their dreams. Perhaps they are afraid of either success or failure. For whatever reason, this is the point where most people fail to consolidate the Leap.

Even if they take the initial Leap, when they are full of excitement and they have not yet faced the fact that this is really going to be different, they fail to take the second Leap.

It is sad to say, but I have seen many people get to this point, and simply stop trying. They go back to their former habits. They stop dreaming. They give up.

Are you going to be that person? Friends, it is easy to have Problem Recognition. (You have to be pretty dense these days if you do not have Problem Recognition!) It isn't too difficult to define your dream. It is not even that difficult to COMMIT to your dreams. (After all, at this stage, you really haven't DONE anything yet.) There are plenty of great people who were just like you, but who made significant changes and overcame the odds. They aren't in your current group of friends probably, but they are out there, and they have systems in place that you can copy. Finding one of them isn't a big chore.

But, executing your plan, actually taking a LEAP, is much more difficult. And, in the end, it is the only step that really matters.

An Author's Note

I know that many of you have read some of my other books. Certainly, almost all of you have read SOME books about motivation and personal growth. So I know that you understand the concept of Leaping. But, I also know that many of you have not made the Leap! Or, if you have, you have not done it again and again until you have reached your dreams.

I want to help you change that situation. I want *this* book to be the beginning of a new life for you. In the next few chapters, I am going to give you some specific instructions for changing your life PERMANENTLY. But, no matter what I show you, or how well I explain it, you are the one who has to do the work. You are the one who has to face your brother-in-law at the dinner table, and you are the one who has to do something different.

If you can face down those fears; if you can say to yourself, "This is my life and I have the power to change it for the better;" if you can somehow find the strength and conviction to work a simple plan, you can succeed where almost none of your family and friends have ever succeeded before.

There is only one thing standing in your way. It is, of course, YOU.

To get past the person that is blocking you (you!), you have to Leap over fears, low energy, risks, friends, family, depression and all the other things that are holding YOU back.

At this point, I am only going to ask you to make a simple resolution. Resolve to define your dreams, and commit to them. In order to do this, you need to write them down here—specifically.

1. Travel several times a year on vacation to different countries, taking in 1 or 2 Grand Slam tennis tournaments along the way

2. Have $100,000 in the checking/savings account at any time, so I never worry about monthly bills

3. Write a $10,000 check to a charity that I really admire

Then, read them to the person who is most important to you in your life, and ask them to help you reach them.

Chapter Five

Before You Leap,
Know Where You Want To Land

> *"All growth is a leap in the dark:*
> *a spontaneous, unpremeditated act*
> *without benefit of experience."*
>
> Henry Miller, Author

*D*id you ever hear the expression, "Look before you leap?" This is great advice, but I have even better advice. "Look at where you intend to land, and then leap to get there."

Folks, it isn't the *leaping* that is important, it is the landing. Leaping is just a way of getting what you want quicker and easier. But, make no mistake about it, the whole reason you are leaping in the first place is because you have a burning desire to land somewhere better. It is one of the things that separates successful Leapers from people who are just jumping in place, going nowhere, but making a lot of commotion and stirring things up. Successful Leapers leap because they want to land someplace special.

And successful Leapers know one very important thing—keep your eyes on the landing spot at all times.

A Leaper Who Landed Where He Was Looking

In 333 B.C., Alexander the Great was 22 years old. He had a huge army, and had an ambition to conquer Asia. But, at that point, he had no significant victories to his name. He needed to do something to prove to both his army and his enemies that he was a man to be reckoned with.

One hundred years before that time, an emperor named Gordius tied his wagon to a post in a town in Macedonia, by using a very complicated knot. Legend had it that the person who could untie the knot would be the next emperor. When Alexander saw the knot, he tried to untie it for hours. He became frustrated, and cried "What does it matter how I loose this knot!" and drew his sword and cut the knot in half.

He went on to conquer the entire known world. Make no mistake about it however, he was not interested in the knot, or the wagon or the rope. He had his eyes on a prize, and didn't want to spend any more time than necessary *attaining* his prize.

You Will "Flip" Over This Example

When a world-class gymnast throws herself into the air at the end of a routine, she is *looking* at the landing spot, even though she is twirling through the air. She knows exactly where she wants to land. She focuses on it, and there is nothing more important to her than "Sticking" the landing. In fact, the judges will often award the gold medal to the person who has the best landing.

Of course, the gymnasts need to do some spectacular Leaping, don't they? But they are all doing the leaping at the same level of difficulty. It is the landing that is the symbol of their success. No gymnast thinks about staying in the air; they all think about where they want to land.

We Aren't Taught To "Stick" A Landing

Almost no one in today's world is taught to "Stick" a landing. Why? Because almost no one is encouraged to leap.

Most of us are taught to plod along, putting one foot in front of the other, keeping in a straight line and doing what we are told. Yet this is a recipe for mediocrity at best and utter failure at worst (and most commonly!). How many times do we hear the words, "Get a good education, get a good job, work hard and you will succeed?" Well, here is a question I would like to ask the people who say that:

"When will we succeed?" How many years does it take for most people to achieve success? Is it 20, 30, 40? How many years must you work, taking one step up the ladder at a time, before you achieve any kind of success?

And, at the end of all that time, what kind of success do most people have? They have a *small* amount of savings, a big mortgage, and they are forced to cut back on all their expenses because they are on a "fixed income." That's it. That is what they get from plodding along for forty or fifty years. That is sad.

The Reason Most People Need To Stick a Landing

If you are a Leaper, it is because you are looking beyond the immediate future, and planning on Sticking a Landing someplace exciting, worthwhile and good. But, the average person is only looking straight ahead. They don't need to plan, because they are only doing what they did the day before, even though it hasn't worked yet. They are thinking, "Okay, what is the next step? When is the next payday, and what do I have to do to hold on to my job so that I can get paid every two weeks?"

The irony is this—these people report to CEOs who have fabulous wealth. The top management at most companies is making a fortune. Yet, they are able to "sell" the idea of working day to day, never thinking about the big picture, to millions of employees around the world.

Why aren't people becoming Leapers and trying to make massive changes in their lives? I think the answer is this—they just don't believe it is possible. They buy into the story they are told, and keep on doing the same thing again and again. They never celebrate Leap Year.

Most people act like they are in a maze. They never see past the next corner. They end up going down blind alleys, ending up with huge obstacles in front of them, unable to find a way around the problems.

Look at the maze below. This is the way that most people conduct their entire lives. They face a maze in grade school, then high school, and maybe even college. When they graduate, they get a job and start all over again. Each day, they get up and follow all the other people, trying to get out of the maze, and into the landing zone.

Here is the problem. They will spend their entire life in the maze. It takes years and years to escape, and many people never find their way out.

Is this what your life is like? Are you stuck in the maze, with no apparent way out? If so, you are not alone, but that is small consolation. Just because you have other people to be miserable with, doesn't mean you aren't miserable!

Leap Out Of the Maze

When you were a kid, did you ever get a book of mazes? You probably did, and you probably spent your time trying to draw a line through the maze. You were careful not to cross any lines, weren't you?

Well, if you listen to the other people, your life will be like this. You will spend your time putting one foot in front of the other, trying to work your way out of the maze by following the prescribed route. You will never move forward quickly, because you are always afraid of going down a blind alley and getting stuck. If you do that, you have to go back and start over again. No one wants that.

This fear keeps you moving slowly and deliberately. You take small steps, always obeying the rules. It takes you forever to get out of the maze—if you ever do.

But, what if you simply leaped out of the maze? What if you simply said, "I don't want to worry about the obstacles and challenges? I just want to jump out of here. I think I will jump over all these walls, and get to the place where I want to be!"

The View Inside

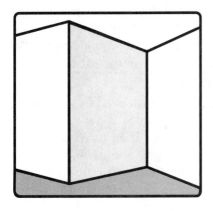

Here is what the maze looks like from the inside. Notice the high walls that block the way. Notice the sharp corners that leave you isolated and alone. This is a sad way to spend a lifetime, but most people do just that.

But remember folks, this is a Leap Year! You can do things you could never do in a regular year. It is a time when women can ask men to marry them, or when you can take a giant leap out of the maze and land on your dreams. Don't let this opportunity slip by!

It Isn't What You Do, It's Where You Look

When I was learning how to golf, I learned a very important point. The ball will go where you look. If you are looking to the right, the ball will go there. If you are looking to the left, the ball will go there. If you look at the hole while you putt, that is where the ball will go. (Okay, maybe golf is a bad example, because the ball never seemed to go anywhere I wanted it to go, but you get my point, don't you?)

In life, if you are looking at the work you have to do tomorrow, that is where you will focus your energy. If, instead, you are looking at the place where you want to live, or the car you want to drive or the college you want to be able to afford to send your kid to, that is where your energy will go. Stop looking at the person ahead of you, and start looking for your dreams.

Focus on your dreams. Focus on the results of hard work, and the maze falls away and you can leap into the spot you want to be. You always need to keep your eyes on your goals. Never worry about the next move, or the next paycheck. Always think about what it is you want, and visualize it. This will help you overcome all the challenges you face.

Where Do You Want To Land?

Remember, this is a Leap Year. You are going to leap over all your challenges and obstacles, and land in your dream space. You will land feet first and stick that landing. When you land in your dream space, the judges will hold up perfect scores, and the crowd will roar with applause and approval.

So where do you want to land? This is an excellent question.

When Jeannie and I decided to change our lives and enjoy our first Leap Year Celebration on July 7, 1993, we were completely focused on the spot where we wanted to stick our landing, not on the things we had to do. Let me refresh your memory and tell you the things we decided we wanted.

1. A nice house on the water
2. A large boat
3. Jeanne to stay home to raise our kids
4. No loss of income; in fact, a gain in income despite the fact that we were living on one salary
5. Time for vacations (and we defined the type, number and length of those vacations)
6. The ability to take care of our parents
7. The ability to pay for college for our kids
8. A car and driver for me
9. And much, much more...

Remember, at the time, I was a college professor. College professors do not have nice homes on the water, a single-income family, a big boat, vacations and the ability to take care of their parents. There was nothing in our experience that screamed, "You can have these things." We couldn't look around and see other college professors who had these things. We needed a break with the past. We needed to *leap*, not take small steps.

But, we didn't look at the next logical step. We looked at the *landing* area where we wanted to be. If we had kept our eyes on the next logical step, we never would have had any of these things. Instead, because we looked at the landing area, we were able to achieve our dreams in about five years. Yes, it was five years of very hard work, but it was worth it.

It Wasn't Just Material Things

When you look at the things I listed above, you shouldn't get confused. We weren't looking for just material things (although I did *love* my boat!). We knew our landing zone would need to be filled with two people (us) who were much different than we were when we were in the maze. We had to grow and change *quickly* so that we could *stick that landing.*

You see folks, if you want to make a big leap, you need to be a different person when you land, or you will never *stick* that landing and hold it. You need to make big changes in the way you treat others, how you view wealth, the world, and how you love. I had to learn to listen to others in order to *stick* my landing which, for me, was a major problem.

The Art of Visualizing the Landing

I will talk about who you must be after a few paragraphs, but first let's talk about visualizing your landing. You need to have very specific goals and dreams. Do not spare the details. There will be many obstacles to your *Leaping and Sticking* the landing. If you do not know exactly what you are trying to accomplish, you will certainly fail.

Write down your goals, and put them on a LARGE piece of paper above the dresser. It can be easy to forget and get discouraged. Not every day will go well while you are leaping. There will be times when it seems difficult to go on.

The only thing that matters is what you want. The only thing that matters is what you can achieve by Leaping, not working for someone else's dreams.

Jeanne and I were so specific that I can still remember some of those dreams almost 20 years later. I remember how many vacations we wanted to take, and what size boat we wanted.

When we landed we stuck the landing, because we always knew exactly what we wanted.

What Are You Leaping Over?

Here is a good question: "What are YOU leaping over?" In other words, what obstacles, difficulties or challenges might be in your path? I made a short list of the things you are most likely to have to deal with ("Leap Over") along the way. If you want to add more, help yourself. I know there are plenty more things you might have to "Leap Over" during your journey:

- Fear
- Envy
- Resentment
- Time problems
- Money problems
- Rejection
- Risk
- Traditions
- Ignorance
- Bad beliefs
- Brothers-in-law, uncles, or other relatives
- Family history
- Culture
- Your boss
- Etc. etc.

These are the things that are in your way right now. They are the walls of the maze that most of us operate in. You must believe that there are thousands and thousands of people who have overcome all of these things. There are thousands and thousands of people who said, "I am not going to walk the same path as everyone else. I am going to focus on the landing zone, and stick my landing when I Leap. I am going to just jump over the obstacles and worry about them later."

Folks, here is a funny thing that I want you to remember. Whenever I said to myself, "I am going to just leap over these obstacles and worry about them later," I never had to worry about them later! It turned out that the things that held me back the most - fear, rejection, misguided self-worth concepts—were NOTHING when I *stuck* my landing. You see, after I Leaped over the obstacles, none of them had a hold on me anymore.

However, if I took my eyes off my landing zone, off my goals, those obstacles would completely run my life. Each one of them had a tremendous hold on me. If I tried to work through them, following the adage, "Get a good education, work hard, wait your turn, etc.," then those obstacles absolutely ruled my life.

How Do You Land and Stick It?

In an earlier chapter, I gave you five steps (stages) that you need to go through. These are the things you need to do to Leap and Stick It. Remember, they are Problem Recognition, Design a Dream, Commit to the Dream, Find People who have already solved your problem, and then Execute a Plan again and again. When you do that, you are able to make giant Leaps that get you out of the maze.

Think about the things we learn in this chapter. The majority of people go through life as if they are in a maze. They only see the things directly ahead of them. To get out of the maze, or reach their reward, they need to follow a long path, with twists and turns.

But, here is all you have to do to Leap. Look for someone who has already leapt out of the maze, and do what they did. Stop looking at the people in the maze with you. They aren't Leaping.

Now, to stick the landing, you need to know exactly what you want. This comes from identifying your dream. Keep your eye on the *landing spot* and never, ever, look at the obstacles. Imagine yourself in the landing spot with the successful people you are copying.

For example, when Jeanne and I wanted to change, we *immediately* moved our eyes away from other college professors. We started looking for people who had what we wanted. We discovered that there were a large number of people who had jobs, but who also had businesses. We started doing what they were doing. Soon, we had what they had.

What was the Leap? We stopped looking for a paycheck, and started looking for an income. Just that one change made a huge difference. How did we *stick* the landing? We carefully projected exactly what it would take for us to make the move to the water. We knew what it would cost to the penny. We visited the areas where we wanted to live, and read the real estate pages. We talked with a realtor, and made numerous trips to the area.

I kept careful track of the extra income I was building up. We stopped spending money on the things that were holding us in place, and started saving money for the things we wanted.

We had a very serious plan, and we stuck to it. We developed discipline. We relied on each other, and never took our eyes off the landing.

When we actually landed, it was no problem to make it *stick*. We landed solidly on our feet, and our kids landed with us!

When I bought our first boat, we paid cash for it. It wasn't a new boat, but it was ours. When we first moved to the water, we actually rented our house, and then bought it from the owners. We built up equity in the house, and then used some of that equity to make the purchase.

Just Like the World-Class Gymnasts, We Practiced the Landing

When you watch a professional gymnast (or a world-class amateur), you see the results of many hours of practice. They don't just run down the mat, leap onto the apparatus, twirl through the air and then *stick* the landing the first time they try something. They break the move down into stages. They practice each one, and they take joy in the perfection of each stage.

Some Leapers (freestyle skiers for example) actually land in water to practice their jumps. They are so busy practicing the take-offs, and the twirls and twists, that they don't even try to stick the landing at first. They know they *eventually* want to stick a landing, but they need to get the rest of their routines under control first.

There are zero gymnasts that can start out with a triple flip with a double twist. They start out with easier techniques, and then progress to the tough stuff.

Jeanne and I didn't make our first Leap and land on the water, with a boat in the backyard. We had to first learn to do the things that Leapers do. We had to learn to let go of the beliefs and practices that held us back. After we had some small success, we were able to work on the big landing.

How Many Leaps Does It Take?

How many times will you need to Leap before you stick your landing in your final goal? It depends entirely on how far it is to your goal! But, no matter what it takes, it will be worth it.

Just do like the great gymnasts do, and start with the basics. Go back to the five-part strategy for Leaping. Always identify the problems, and then build your dream. Make the commitment, find the people who already did it and then execute that plan of yours again and again.

If you do all those things, I promise you it will work. How do I know? How can I make that promise? We were an unlikely couple for success. We were brought up to believe a certain tradition. When we needed to leap, we were leaping from a place where almost all of my colleagues were stuck fast. Our Leap was so far that it was really hard to even imagine the landing spot, let alone visualize ourselves there. Nobody we knew at the time had done it.

And, remember, I am legally blind. Who would think that someone with a handicap like that would be able to produce a stream of income to move to the water and have a big boat?

We did it by practicing the basics, putting it all together, keeping an eye on the landing spot and following the lead of people who had already solved the problem.

Are you ready to stick it?

In this chapter, we talked about the "maze" which is really comprised of all your obstacles. In order to make the leap, and stick the landing, you need to identify the challenges you face. In the space below, list the things that are holding you back. Use the list from the chapter to get you started. Now, resolve to overcome them, because you will soon find that they become meaningless when you move past them.

Chapter Six

Are You Worth It?

"An optimist stays up until midnight to see the New Year in. A pessimist stays up to make sure the Old Year leaves."

Bill Vaughan, Author and Comedian

There is one thing we can say about Leapers—they are valuable people. However, they aren't valuable because of the amount of money they have, or the things they own. Yes, money, nice possessions, a comfortable lifestyle and freedom from worry are all *outward signs* of value. Leapers are valuable because they CREATE THE VALUE through their actions and attitudes, their beliefs and their convictions.

And, because they are so valuable, they are worth it!

When Is Someone "Worth It?"

People are always questioning their value to others. Indeed, most people spend their whole lives under-valuing their personal worth. This under-valuation is reflected in the way most people give up their dreams early in life, in order to live "in the real world". Look at the pictures to see exactly what I mean.

How Leapers Think

Dreams

Reality

Develop BIG Dreams,
then expand your reality.

What most people do

Dreams

Reality

Shrink your dreams,
to fit into a small reality.

Here's what most people do, and it is why they under-value themselves. They look at their present situation, and think of it as a permanent reality. They are caught in the maze, and taking one step at a time. They can't see past the obstacles in front of them. They waste time going down blind alleys in the maze, and never look over the walls to see what is on the outside of the maze. They follow everyone else.

Then, they make the fatal mistake. They shrink their dreams to fit into the "reality," instead of expanding their reality to accommodate their dreams. (See the pictures) This error in judgment condemns them to a lifetime of undervalued existence. Isn't it amazing that one concept should have such a profound effect?

The Price of Shrinking Your Dreams

I don't think most people realize the exact cost of shrinking their dreams. It is massive. It is a daily cost. If you undervalue yourself by $5 on day 1, you will live with that cost every day for the rest of your life. On day 2, you are now up to a $10 cost. Over a year, it costs $1,825—unless it is a LEAP year, when it costs you $1,830!

However, this assumes you do not make any *other* under-valuations. If you make a second mistake, even if it only costs you $5 per day, you will soon be losing $3,660 per Leap Year. But, let's face it. Most people don't undervalue themselves by just $10 per day. No, most people are letting hundreds of dollars per day escape, day-by-day for a lifetime. What is the value of that thinking?

Folks, the mistake comes *directly* from assuming the present situation is the reality you must live with. It is not; it is merely the situation you created so far. It can change at any time, because you are the one who created it. Every reality is the direct consequence of how you believe and act; no one else controls your reality.

The Definition of Price

Most people think of price as the "price tag." They look at a new coat, for example, and immediately search for the price tag on the sleeve. But price is much more than just the price tag. I want you to look at price as marketers see it. Here is their definition:

Price is everything you give up to get what you want.

If you think of price this way, you will soon see how costly it is to undervalue yourself. When you accept the present situation as a permanent reality, you must give up your dreams! This is a horrifying price to pay for a simple mistake. When you give up your dreams, or shrink them to fit into the "reality," you are paying a price for that every day for the rest of your life, and that price is compounding, just like some hideous interest payment.

You Control Your Reality

Do you believe me when I say that you control your own reality? I suppose it depends on how you answer the age-old question, "Do you see the glass as half-empty, or half-full?" Your attitudes, your beliefs, and your subsequent actions will determine whether you control your reality, or if you are going to turn it over to someone else. I prefer to control my own reality.

Because of my limited eyesight, people are always saying to me, "How do you do it? How do you write all those books and travel around the world giving talks?" These questions always astonish me because, for me, there is no choice. I have BIG DREAMS and I will do whatever it takes to reach them. In fact, my family motto is, "The least I will do is whatever it takes."

Would I have an excuse to shrink my reality to fit my dreams? Some people would think so; I do not. I am too busy expanding my reality to *accommodate* my dreams. I hire drivers and traveling companions, work with editors on my books, work longer hours to do all the writing, etc. I simply do "Whatever it takes" to reach my dreams.

However, without those dreams, I would not have the ability, or the energy, to change my reality. Without the dreams, there would be no driving force that helps me overcome the depression that sometimes sets in when I can't see something that everyone else sees.

Ironically, however, because of my dreams, I see things that no one else sees. I see the rewards for being a Leaper. I see the rewards for making every year a Leap Year, instead of a common year.

I challenge you to do the same thing. I know you have problems; we all do. But, stop paying the terribly high price of shrinking those dreams (or abandoning them altogether) because you feel that your present situation is your permanent reality.

The Price Our Children Pay

It is bad enough that we undervalue ourselves and pay a terrible price. However, we're passing along this same disastrous belief system to our kids. Although we may be trying to protect them by teaching them to lower their expectations, it is a stunningly harmful practice.

When our children say, "I can't wait to grow up and have a big house, with lots of cars and all the money I want," we patiently smile to ourselves and think, "It is good for them to feel this way. When they get a little older, I'll tell them what really happens." As the kids get older, we slowly but surely start to send them messages. We want to lower their expectations until we get them to a point where they will not be disappointed.

When they say, *"Let's take a big vacation this year; we can all go someplace together,"* we say, *"We can't afford that; besides, I have to work."*

When they say, *"Well, when I grow up, I am going to take a big vacation every year, and spend time with my kids,"* we say, *"No, people like us can't do that. If you want things you can't have, you will always be disappointed. You should learn to live within your means. People who want too much are never happy. You want to be happy, don't you?"*

Can you see what we're doing? Can you see how we're trying to lower expectations so that kids won't be sad because they can't afford things? Yet, this is **EXACTLY** why people under-value themselves. It is **EXACTLY** why they accept a job rather than creating a lifestyle. We don't want our children to get hurt, but by lowering expectations, we pass along one of the most harmful sets of attitudes and beliefs possible.

The Stunning Secret of your Worth

I am about to share the most incredible information you are likely to get. In a few paragraphs, you will learn why you are being under-valued, and why it will continue forever. I hope you are ready for this information because, once you understand it, you will have to make a decision. Once you learn that you are *permanently* undervalued, you will have a clear choice—let it continue, or do something about it. But, make no mistake, when this secret is revealed to you, you will have to make that choice, and it might be painful.

Here is the secret:

Somewhere, there is a man or woman with a dream, and the will to achieve it. He/She becomes a Leaper, and builds a company to achieve the dream. The Leaper hires employees, and pays them to work. What are the employees paid to do? They are paid to help the Leaper achieve his/her dream! Employees are never paid enough to achieve their own dreams, because this would not leave enough money left over for the Leaper to achieve his/her dream. The difference between what the employees get paid, and the Leaper retains, is the price of a dream.

Do you see what we are saying here? When we ask "Are You Worth It?" you have to answer the question like this:

"I am worth it to the person who pays me, because they are paying me less than what I am worth!" This may be a little difficult to live with, but it is the truth. Just because it isn't pleasant doesn't make it less true.

What You Are Given Is Worth Less

Here is something to remember: "What you are *given* is always worth less than what you *create*." If you wait for someone to give you something, instead of creating what you need, you will always get less. Why is this true? The answer is another great secret of economic life. You are given money for the value you add, and nothing more. If you add a lot of value, you get a lot of money. If you add just a little value, you get less. But, in any case, the money an employee gets is always worth less than the value they produce. Here is why:

Let's say a woman named Marie has a dream. She wants to have money, and the time to spend it (lifestyle!) Marie is a great baker, so she sets up a Cake and Pie business. Her desserts are so good that soon she has too many orders to handle. She hires an assistant to do the baking.

Why is Marie able to sell her pies and cakes for a profit? She *adds value* to the raw ingredients. She buys fruit, flour and other ingredients from a supplier, and then *adds value* by combining them and baking them with care and diligence. She also *adds value* by doing all the work, and then delivering the desserts to the party or special occasion on time. Marie makes her money by *selling the added value to the customer*. In other words, *whatever added value she creates, she can sell.*

Marie had so many orders that she hired an assistant to do the baking. "Doing the baking" was one of the things Marie did to add value, right? Okay, so if she wants to make money from that added value, she has to pay the assistant less than the value of the work! (By the way, this is where money comes from in almost any business.)

Marie is able to achieve her dreams, but the assistant will always get less. If the assistant had his/her own business, then the assistant could get paid the full value of the work. Whenever you are *given* something, it is always worth less than when you *create* it.

Does this make sense to you? Can you see what I am trying to tell you? If you work for someone else, if you trade your time for dollars, you will always be under-valued. When I ask you, "Are You Worth It?" you will have to say, "NO!" Every day of your life, you are giving away money. Every day of your life, you are paying a price for doing the same thing that nearly everyone else is doing. You are paying a terrible price, because *price is everything you give up to get what you want,* and you are giving up your dreams!

And, as we discussed, through both your beliefs and your *example,* you are teaching your children to give up their dreams. Each new generation gives up more and more. When I ask you, "Are You Worth It?" you can say, "No." When I ask your children, they will have to say, "No Way!"

And Now, YOUR CHOICE

Earlier in this chapter, I warned you that you would need to make a choice. I warned you that you would discover some information that would force you into the choice. You see folks, once you know this big secret, you are in a difficult spot. You now know that you are under-valued, and that it is costing you a terrible price. You also know exactly HOW this under-valuing works. And, you know now that you are passing along this practice to your children.

Before you knew this information, perhaps you might have talked yourself into believing that everything was "as good as it should be." But now you know that you have consistently shrunk your dreams (or given them up altogether) in order to meet your reality. By now, you should completely understand that you have absolute control over your reality, and not the other way around. And finally, you are aware that you are passing along terrible examples and lessons to your children.

And, when you know these things, when they are plainly evident to you, you can no longer ignore them and pretend that you are Worth It.

So, now you have a choice. Do you change, or do you continue on your present course? When I ask you, "Are You Worth It?" will you answer "No" or "Yes?" Or, will you say, "It doesn't look like I am Worth It, but I am ready to change!"

If you are ready to change, and change the fortunes of your family for generations, then you are ready to proceed. When you begin to make Leaps, you begin to increase your worth—on many levels.

When we are children, we have grand dreams about doing something exciting, living in a great home, and having time to do whatever we want. However, as time goes on, we realize that those dreams may not be attainable. We begin to fall prey to one of the most harmful beliefs in the world. Do you know what it is? It is, *"People like me don't get to make choices. We go to work, and work hard. We ask our bosses for a raise, and if he/she doesn't give it to us, we go without."* We teach our children to accept this status. Our children say, *"Someday, I am going to live in a big house and spend all my time with my kids, going fishing, or playing with them or doing things like that. I will make a lot of money and be able to buy all the things I want."* We try not to kill their dreams, but we also need to teach them the valuable lessons of the real world.

These lessons are not lost on the kids, who grow up learning to under-value themselves. The vast majority of people just *accept* what they are given. Of course, the amount that someone else gives you is worth well below the amount you are worth!

And so it goes. The cycle continues; the trap stays secure. Each generation teaches the next to take one step at a time, and to accept their fate. This is Feudalism in the twenty-first century. This goes on and on, until each generation dies out, or…

UNTIL SOMEONE LEARNS TO LEAP! The only way the cycle can be broken is if someone is brave enough to become a Leaper, to think differently, to recognize that there is a problem, to build a dream and commit to it and to find people who have already solved the problem. In fact, it will continue in YOUR family unless you shout "Happy Leap Year" right now and then take a Leap!

Happy Leap Year!

For this resolution, I want you to estimate how much you are losing each day because you are under-valued. How do you do this? First, estimate how much money you would need to make each year to live the way you really would like to live. Then, subtract the money you make now. Divide the results by 366. This is how much you are under-valued each day. It is the money you should be making in order to achieve your dreams.

Now, resolve to do whatever it takes to make up the difference.

Chapter Seven

How to Develop Leaping Leverage

> *"It is a truly wise man who does not play Leap Frog with a unicorn."*
>
> Unknown

*I*n the Spring of 1967, as a high-school freshman, I did something remarkable. At a track meet, I jumped higher than Russian Valeriy Brumel, the World Record holder at that time. The World's High Jump record was 7 feet, 6 inches, and had actually been set in 1963. That is a High Jump indeed! Imagine running up to a bar and leaping into the air like that. That height was at least a full foot taller than Brumel.

So how did I, a skinny kid from Philadelphia, jump higher than the mighty Russian? It was simple really; I was a *pole-vaulter!* I was able to jump higher because I had leverage. In fact, all of the pole-vaulters I knew were able to out-leap the best high jumpers.

We had to practice, of course. Pole-vaulting is tricky. But, it propelled us to greater heights than the world's best high jumpers.

Sometimes, Leverage is just Luck

I remember the day I became a pole-vaulter. I had done well on the cross-country running team in the fall of my freshman year, so it was natural that I go out for track. Our track coach had recently retired, so the football coach, "Tex" Flannery, had the honors. Our school was an all-boys academy, and Coach Flannery enlisted the help of a local college coach to help with the field events. He was a Christian Brother named Brother Luke. Brother Luke assembled the freshmen on the field and asked, "Does anyone want to do the long jump?" I knew that wasn't going to be my event, and besides, I was a runner. I waited for more announcements. He went through them all—shot-put, definitely not discus (what was *that?*), javelin (*I was more into fishing than throwing a spear*), *and finally, the magic words, "Does anyone want to be a pole-vaulter?"*

BINGO. No one in my family had been a pole vaulter. In fact, I had never really even thought much about it. But it looked very cool, and here was Brother Luke asking for *volunteers*. He wasn't saying, "Who wants to *try out* to be a pole vaulter?" He was just offering it up, and I took the offer in a heartbeat.

So, how did I become a pole vaulter? It was just plain luck. I was in the right place at the right time. Nobody else stepped forward.

What I Learned About Leverage

I am not going to tell you that I was *terrific* at the sport. I can say that I was the best freshman on the team. Of course, I was the only freshman on the team, but that is beside the point.

Here is the point. No matter if you are a good pole vaulter, or a mediocre one, the very first thing you realize is that you are going to jump higher with a pole than you ever could without one. The pole gives you leverage. It requires some effort from the vaulter, but the effort is small in comparison to the results.

But, while I learned that using the pole gave me super human leaping ability, there were certain things you had to do in order for the leverage to work. For example, if you weren't moving down the runway at high speeds, you couldn't get up enough speed to use the pole. Instead of soaring up and over the bar, you just soared up, and then came back down in the wrong place—behind where you started the jump!

On the other hand, if you jumped in the wrong place, you completely missed the soft landing area. That was even worse, because you were really flying at that point, and the ground *around the pit* was very hard.

Now, as I said, I wasn't a great pole vaulter, but I did learn how to do it, and I did have some success. I was better than many pole vaulters, and I was far better than all the high jumpers.

Would You Like Leverage?

You could become very good at Leaping, and have a very Happy Leap Year. By learning to look at the world differently and do things other people will not do, you can Leap your way into better health, happiness and wealth; you could become the very best Leaper you can be—or in the world.

However, if you Leap without Leverage, almost every *Leveraged Leaper* is going to do better than you. Even a mediocre *Leveraged Leaper* can out-Leap a non-leveraged Leaper (Try reading that last sentence out loud quickly!)

I assume that you are an ordinary person—much like me. You have determination, some mental ability, a reasonable personality and maybe even a gift for communicating (I am also devilishly handsome, or at least *I* think so.)

Folks, even ordinary people like you and me can learn to achieve great things by leveraging our leaps. You see, unlike the leap itself, leveraging takes almost no additional effort. In fact, once you learn a few basic techniques, a leveraged Leap is much easier than a regular Leap.

In addition, it is fun. You become a bit of a celebrity. That was one of the things I liked most about pole vaulting. It was different, and people knew it. Anyone can run around a track, but how many of us can grab a 15-foot pole and soar (sort of) over a bar into a soft pit lined with foam rubber?

When you take your first Leap, you will be different. And then, when you take your first Leveraged Leap, you will be strikingly different—and the rewards will be as well.

How Do You Leverage Your Leaps?

If you want to be a *Leveraged Leaper,* you should understand two things to leverage. They are time and money.

All business success is based on using *inputs* to produce *outputs.* The idea is to put in as few inputs, and to take out as many outputs as possible. The only way to decrease inputs and, at the same time, to increase outputs, is to use leverage.

Are you beginning to see the framework here? Can you envision where we are about to go? I hope so but, if not, don't worry. Just read on and all will become clear.

Time and Money – Inputs and Outputs

In business, we use two resources (time and money) and we produce two resources (time and money). The goal is to get the most out, while putting the least in.

If you have a job, you are putting a lot of time into producing a limited amount of money. I say "limited" because you can only make so much. If you are trading *your* time alone, then you have a limited amount to put into the job. You get paid on a one-to-one basis.

If you have a traditional business, you are putting a lot of both time and money into the business, but the possible rewards are larger. Of course, the possible *failures* are also greater.

In a traditional business you do have leverage, because you are hiring other people to do the work. But remember, you are also inputting a lot of both time and money. Do you have a lot of time and money to put into your endeavor? I don't, because I am an ordinary person; I don't want to risk my time and money. Instead, I would rather *leverage* it.

The questions, of course, are, "How do I leverage my Leaps?" and, "What can an ordinary person do in this troubled economic climate to create a better life through leverage?"

These are great questions, and while I am going to provide answers throughout this book, let me address some basic strategies here.

1. **Decrease your input**—Focus on your dreams, and you will limit the input you waste

2. **Value your time**—Most of us put more value on money. However, *the minute you start valuing time,* you automatically produce more

3. **Focus on creating equity**—let the equity do the work. This decreases inputs and increases outputs. (More on this in the chapter "Do You Own Your Life Or You Just Renting?")

4. **Pay others to do the things you don't have time to do**— Don't use the excuse, "I don't have time to pursue my dreams." Pay others to do the things you don't want to do, and focus on the important, output-producing things that you *must* do to achieve your dreams

5. **Do *exactly* what successful people are doing**—They already figured it out. Adopt their habits, and follow their system. It will save you time and money, and *produce* time and money

Leveraged Leaping for the Ordinary Man and Woman

Here is the dilemma. The majority of us are never going to get ahead, because we are always trying to follow a model that is designed to keep us on a certain track. In this book, you will learn how the common wisdom that tells us to, "Get a good education, get a good job and work hard" is fundamentally flawed. It is fine if you want to work hard for the rest of your life and end up in debt, asking the government for money. Actually, the system works just fine for that. But, for the ordinary man or woman who wants extraordinary outcomes, this is no way to go through life.

The best way for ordinary men and women to learn to Leap and Leverage is to open your mind to a new way of thinking. When Brother Luke said, "Who wants to be a pole-vaulter?," I was open to the message. Remember, before that, I had spent my track time running around a quarter-mile oval. When you run around a track, do you know where you are when you finish a race? You are right back where you started from!

There are no big secrets to learning to acquire Leaping Leverage; it is really quite simple. After all, I did it, and I am nobody special. I have friends who did it and, believe me, *they* are nobody special!

In recent years, I have watched countless people make incredible changes in their lives. I can tell you this; none of them did it by following the old rules. Each of them made a specific decision, and each of them used leverage. When the recent recession began, and the unemployment rate in the United States shot through the roof, anyone who was dependent on a single source of income was IMMEDIATELY in trouble. Yet, how many of those people made fundamental changes? The answer, sadly, is that very few did. This means the next time we have a downturn (and it could happen anytime) they will be in the same dangerous situation.

Would it matter if I told them, "You need to develop Leaping Leverage so that you do not get in trouble again" if they were not ready to hear the message? Of course it wouldn't.

Most of the people you know are not going to make changes in their lives. Even though they have just seen the near collapse of our economic model, they will not change. They won't change even if *you* are able to change. WHY? Well, most people are simply not looking for change. They want the world to change to suit them. They want to believe that the system we have been taught to follow will someday, somehow, magically work.

I will tell you the one thing you need to do to create a better life. When Brother Luke (or whoever it turns out to be) comes up to you and says, "Would you like to be a wealthy, happy, stress-free person?" you have to be ready to say, "That sounds great! Let's do it."

Don't Forget To Run

Earlier in this chapter, I told you what I learned about using the pole to leverage my Leaps. Let me remind you again.

Run at top speed—You need some speed in order to Leap! While you are limiting your input, you have to remember that no-one else is going to be excited about the process unless you are running and leaping at your top speed. Be a great example, and others may follow. Move too slowly, and you will fall down on the wrong side of the bar.

Your momentum is very important. It will not only carry you to your goals, it will inspire others to Leverage their Leaps as well.

Do I still Pole Vault?

Are you kidding me? Of course not. But, I still think like a pole-vaulter! In my mind at least, I am still running down that runway, pole in hand, looking for that feeling of exhilaration as I go higher than anyone else has ever gone in the history of the world—if they are not using a pole.

How about you? Would you like to join me?

If you do not have the things you want in life, it is probably because you are doing the wrong things to try to get them. At this point, you may need to do something completely different, completely unexpected.

You may need to become a pole vaulter! Will you be ready?

In the space below, write a statement that tells the world you will be open to new possibilities. Resolve to stay alert, and to listen to opportunities—especially from people who have what you want.

Chapter Eight

Do You Own Your Life,
or Are You Just Renting

> *"I advise you to say your dream*
> *is possible and then overcome all*
> *inconveniences, ignore all the hassles,*
> *and take a running leap through the*
> *hoop even if it is in flames."*
>
> Les Brown, Author and Speaker

What Separates the Poor from the Wealthy, and the Owners from the Renters?

Here is something that no one will teach you in school. How do I know this? I am a college professor, and most of the people I work with have never heard of this concept—even business professors. You can spend your whole life renting your job, or your business, and never build equity in either. At the end of your life, you have nothing of value. But, more tragically, during your life, while you were working so hard, you had nothing of value either.

Own, Don't Rent

Too many people go through life without owning a thing. They don't own their homes (the bank owns it), they don't own their jobs (they have no equity in the company) and they don't even own their futures, because their lives are controlled by others. Let me give you an example of just such a person:

Robert was a very wealthy man, but he was so busy that he never had time to enjoy his wealth. One day his favorite uncle died, and Robert decided to give him an outstanding funeral. However, he was going away on a business trip, so he called the funeral director with the following request:

"I want you to give my uncle a first-class funeral," he said. "Spare no expense and send me the bill. I will be on a business trip, so I won't be able to attend personally."

The company gave Robert's uncle the best funeral money could buy, and sent Robert a bill for $45,000. Robert was a little stunned by the amount, but everyone who was in attendance told him it was a real tribute to the uncle, and a fine funeral. Robert paid the bill.

One month later, he got another bill from the Funeral Home for $325. Robert was very confused, but he was so busy that he just paid it. One month later, another bill for $325 arrived, and again he paid it.

This went on for six months, and Robert finally took the time to call the funeral home to ask them why he was getting monthly bills for $325.

"You told us you wanted this funeral to be first-class, didn't you?" asked the funeral director. "Yes, I did," Robert said, "but I paid you $45,000 after the service. Why am I still getting this monthly bill?"

"The answer is simple," said the director, "we wanted him to look good in the coffin, so we rented him a tuxedo."

Now, I am certain that most of us would never do anything this foolish, would we? But, how many of us are trapped in an endless cycle of payments for the things we *think* we own, but are really renting?

Life on the Treadmill

Robert Kiyosaki, author of *Rich Dad, Poor Dad*, describes the typical person's life as a treadmill. According to Mr. Kiyosaki, we get a job and get paid, then buy things on credit. Now, we have to work just to pay the interest on our purchases. When we get a raise at work, we buy more things on credit. This means we have to work harder, and make more money. The treadmill begins to speed up. As we make more, and spend more, the treadmill keeps getting faster, and we can't get off.

It Is a Raise and Rent, Raise and Rent Cycle

Do you see how this problem works? For example, if someone makes $50,000 per year they buy a home, a car and other things on credit. Most of their paychecks go to the interest payments on these things.

If they get a $5,000 raise (10%) they think, "Wow, now I can get a better car—one that has more status (or horsepower, or is faster, or…) However, instead of saving up for ten years to buy the car, this person buys it on credit, using the money from the raise. Sure, he pays off a few thousand dollars per year of principal, but the car is depreciating at the same time!

This puts us into a "raise & rent" situation. We do it for all kinds of things. This is why I say, "Most people are just renting their lives."

Is This Any Way to Live?

Of course, most people do not believe that this is a good way to live, but almost everyone in the civilized world is living this way —especially Americans! It is how we buy a house we can't afford, cars that are too expensive, country club membership and college educations - almost everything! There are even some people who use their credit cards to buy groceries.

Of course, all of this would be fine if we could depend on our jobs to keep bringing in the extra money each month to pay for all the interest on our purchases. However, after the last great recession, does anyone think they can depend on their incomes from a job? Even if you do not get laid-off, you may certainly face a salary reduction. How will you pay for your rented life if you don't make as much money as before?

Own, Don't Rent

The solution, of course, is to own things. But, in our economy, is this really possible? What happens if you get laid-off? Even if you made great plans, can you say for certain that you will have a job for the next thirty years while you pay off that mortgage?

In this chapter I am not advising you to *not seek* a mortgage. My purpose is not to tell you to pay cash for your next car, or washing machine, or vacation. This chapter is designed to point out the great HOLE you are digging by renting your life instead of owning it.

It isn't a matter of buying fewer things on credit, although that is a darn good idea. No, to really own your life, you must learn the one great secret of ownership; you need to develop equity!

What Is Equity?

In accounting terms, equity is something you own. However, in "Happy Leap Year" terms, where we want you to make a giant leap forward this year, we define equity as "Something you own that makes money."

You see folks, many people think that owning a home gives them equity. Technically, it does. However, your home is not *making* you money. It does not produce income. Yes, the home can increase in value (well, maybe not!) but it does not *make* money for you. It is an expense, not an income producer.

No, to make a *leap* forward this year, you need to learn to produce equity that makes money for you. You need to cash in on one of the best kept secrets of the wealthy. You don't want to rent your life; you want to own it through equity.

Back to the Treadmill

Let's go back to the treadmill example. Our $50,000/year employee gets a $5,000/year raise. He buys a new car, and his raise pays off the interest. He is renting the car.

However, what if he took that raise money and *invested* it into something that actually makes money instead? For example, instead of buying a new car, suppose he lent the money to a man who buys a taxicab? The man who buys the cab pays our smart executive interest on the loan, plus a percentage of the cab fares. The cab driver works with an established company, and this *leverages* the investment even more. (I am not suggesting that you do this, I am just using it as an example of how the same money can be used to buy something equity-draining, or equity-building.) He *leverages* his time because he buys into a system, and that system has value, and it makes him more money.

Yes, he drives his current car for a few more years but, eventually, he is able to pay cash for a new car, because the money from his *investment* (his equity) creates cash flow. Soon, instead of being trapped on the treadmill, he is taking more vacations, spending more time with his family and doing the things that only people with equity income can do.

Don't Buy Debt, Buy Time

Do you see the difference between someone who rents their life, and someone who owns it through equity? If you trade your time for dollars on a job, you have to spend time to make money. When you build equity, the *equity* does the work and makes the money. Now, you can have the things you want, and the time to enjoy them.

This is the real secret of equity income; recurring income. It works *for* you. You are now the owner, and the equity is now the worker. Building equity, and using it to pay off debt, takes you off the treadmill.

What Exactly Is Equity?

You already know that equity is something you own, and that equity income is recurring, meaning it keeps on coming in, even when you are not actively working. But, what is equity? What are some examples of equity that ordinary men and women can earn, and more importantly, use?

There are five kinds of equity, and each one of them is a great way to produce income and buy back your life. If you use all five, you will quickly learn how to get off the treadmill, have more time, and have more income. When you start to do this, you are making a Leap. The five equities are:

1. **Customer Equity**
2. **System Equity**
3. **Network Equity**
4. **Investment Equity**
5. **Mentor Equity**

Here is a brief explanation of each type of equity, and how it can help you make a Giant Leap this year:

Customer Equity—If you own a business—even if it is a very small business and you operate it from home part-time, you will have customers. They don't appear by magic, you work to get them. They are customers because they buy *something* from you or your company. Even though it takes some work to find customers, it doesn't take as much time to *keep customers. For example, if your customer buys $30 in products the first month, and it took you five hours of work to find that customer and get them to make the first purchase, you do not make much per hour, do you? However, if that customer **automatically reorders** the product the second month, and you did NO work for it, then you made a LOT more per hour the second month, didn't you?* This is customer equity. When you invest time in developing customers, and they reorder, you are creating recurring income. In other words, your customer equity went to work for you and made you money in the second month. If your customer keeps buying again and again, your customer equity continues to generate income for you.

System Equity—Earlier in this chapter, I used the example of the man who bought the taxicab, and then placed it into an existing *system* to leverage his investment. I don't care what you do; there are systems everywhere for you to follow. When I identified the five steps you should follow to make positive Leaps, one of them was "Find people who have already solved your problem, and do what they did". This is a system. Systems are one of the most valuable equities you can own because they are inexpensive (sometimes they are free), and they help you leverage your investment. They save time and make money.

Network Equity—Unlike System Equity, which is already built for you, you might have to build Network Equity. This is your series of personal connections that support your efforts to create wealth and change lives. Network Equity is extremely valuable, and very income-productive. In many ways, network equity is like customer equity. You spend time in the beginning building it, and then get to reap the rewards for a lifetime. Network Equity is a give-and-take relationship. You must continually add to the network. However, the incredible leveraging effects are so powerful that they far outweigh any investment you make—either in terms of time or money. To build your Network Equity, live by the adage, "Give others what they want, and you will get what you want." In many ways, this kind of equity means taking your eyes off your own problems and challenges, and focusing on helping others achieve theirs. If you are building the right kind of network, you are virtually assured that you will find what you want by helping others.

Investment Equity—There are really two kinds of Investment Equity. The first kind is the traditional equity. It may be stocks or bonds, or perhaps even real estate. Most people think of these kinds of investments when they hear the words "Equity". I am totally in favor of making investments in traditional equity. However, in the course of many years of investing, I believe it is not much different than going to Las Vegas and betting on the throw of the dice! Stocks can go up or down. You can win, or you can lose. I prefer the kind of Investment Equity that comes from investing in my personal business. It may be in training, or tools, or some other kind of growth-oriented investment. Perhaps it is a new computer, or some kind of assistant to help me take care of my business needs. Whatever it is, all these investments are goal-oriented. In other words, I make investments that are designed to help me grow my business and, in turn, create even more equity.

Of course, none of us has unlimited funds, so all these investments are made *instead* of buying "things" like new cars. In the end, the recurring income from investment equity will buy something much more valuable than a new car. It will buy freedom. Once we are free, then we can spend the money on a new car.

Mentor Equity—now *this* is big time equity. This is something that no one else can buy or take away from you. You cannot lose Mentor Equity (unlike the other equities). You get mentor equity from two things—Training and Experience. You can get training anywhere. Someone is always willing to train you. After all, they are selling *their* Mentor Equity during the training session. However, experience only comes from trial and error. To gain experience, you must actually do something.

I pour my Mentor Equity into my books and other training programs. People pay me well for it. What kind of Mentor Equity do you have? What kind of training and experience combinations do you have that others will pay you for?

The beauty of Mentor Equity is that it is more valuable now than it was yesterday. Sell it dearly, but do sell it to others. It is a great way to leverage all your work.

One way to build Mentor Equity is to keep a journal, or blog about your experience. Neither of them costs any money to do, yet the powerful effect after some years of practice is incredible.

Remember this about Mentor Equity. It is one of the few things that older people have that younger people think is valuable! But, younger people can have Mentor Equity as well. It all depends on how well you can position your expertise in the minds of others.

A Leap Year of Equity

In the coming Leap Year, you need to concentrate on building equity. It will save you time and money, and it will MAKE you both time and money. In fact, if you get nothing more from this book, please remember to build equity. It is the one thing that will define and differentiate you from the crowd. It will turn a common year into an uncommon celebration. It will bring on a time when you LEAP into a new level of wealth.

Equity Is Leverage

Here is the real beauty of equity and leverage. The right kind of equity *leverages your time and money* and produces more time and money—without additional work from you. This is what you need to do to create a Happy Leap Year.

You still have to apply yourself to make leverage work. If you want to use a lever to move a big rock, you still have to lean on the end of the lever. However, the amount of work you need to do is far less than the results you get.

On July 7, 1993, at 2:30 in the afternoon, when I decided to change my life, the most important decision I made was to identify ways to *leverage* my time and money. When you build equity, it makes money for you, even when you are not working. This is leverage. I didn't want to spend so much time working that I could not enjoy my fishing boat. I didn't want to move to the water and never see my family. I made a nice Leap because I stopped thinking about trading time for dollars, and started building equity so that it could make money for me.

Own Your Life

The most important thing you can do is to take back ownership of your life. You will be amazed at the difference it makes. I am not telling you to throw away your job and start working for yourself full time. I am telling you to protect your primary source of income, but start building equity on the side.

Someday, you may decide to become a full-time entrepreneur, and to live entirely on your equity and leverage. However, most of you will not go that route. Most of you will use equity to create a *cushion* that gives you the extra income you need when times are good and a fall-back position when times are bad.

If you can use the money you create to pay off some of your loans and debts, and if you can create recurring income that keeps coming in, even when you are not working, then you have equity, leverage and COMFORT.

In this book, we talk about establishing your dream, then working to achieve it. You need equity to achieve a big, worthwhile dream. Without it, you are simply renting your life.

This year, resolve to build equity. In the space below, write down the five kinds of equity (found in this chapter). Now, specifically describe the opportunities you have RIGHT NOW to start increasing each of those equities.

Chapter Nine

Would You Rather Own Half A Watermelon, or A Whole Grape?

> *"It doesn't work to leap a twenty foot chasm in two ten foot jumps."*
>
> Anonymous

Do you like the title to this chapter? I do, of course, or I wouldn't have used it. But, I think it brings up a major point that is crucial for anyone who wants to have a Happy Leap Year. If you want to build, if you want to grow wealthy, if you want to create a fabulous lifestyle and make a real difference in this life, you are going to have to *share*.

On Again, Off Again

You should be used to the concept of sharing. After all, when you were a child, your mother surely taught you how important it is to share, didn't she? Can't you just visualize the scene? You are a small child, playing in the sandbox. Your best friend _____ (go ahead, put your best friend's name here) is sitting across from you, and there are two shovels. What would happen if you took both shovels, one for each hand, and _____ didn't have any? You know **EXACTLY** what would happen. _____ would start to cry, and your mother would come out of the house and say to you, "Be a good boy (girl) and share! You wouldn't like it if ____ did the same thing to you, would you?"

Of course, five minutes later, _____ would take both shovels, and YOU would be crying. However, the lesson would stick with you. Sharing is the right thing to do.

Then you got older, and sharing became less important. Soon, you got a job, and you were really getting selfish. Now there wasn't enough to go around. If someone else got the job, you got nothing. If someone else got the raise, or the promotion, you got nothing. Suddenly, sharing didn't seem like such a good idea. Instead, you competed for a limited resource. And, in the end, someone was left in the sandbox crying.

I Am Not a Socialist

Don't get me wrong. I am not advocating a socialistic state where the people who work hard have to share with the people who do not work at all. In fact, I am a true believer in Capitalism, and I always spell it with a capital "C." But I am a believer in sharing, and I love to work in teams of people who strengthen each other, and produce more than the individuals could alone.

I love the idea of sharing excitement, fun, motivation, dreams, work, and most of all, I love the idea of sharing REWARDS.

On the other hand, I want to share the rewards according to results, not effort. It doesn't matter to me how hard someone *tries* to achieve something. I want to share the winnings with other winners, and I want to share them proportionally. Let she who wins the most, receive the most. But let's be certain that he who wins a little gets a little something.

For those who don't try, and don't win, I want to offer my help to change their outcomes. I am always willing to assist someone when they need it. But, they have to recognize that they need it!

Do you remember my discussion of the "Five Step Process for Leaping" in Chapter Four? I wrote about the need for Problem Recognition. Too many people want to get rewards without ever admitting they have a problem to solve first. This is certainly one thing that differentiates me from a socialist. Socialists never require anyone to admit there is a problem (other than the fact that they do not have enough money!) Further, I require that people commit to their dreams and follow a system before they earn my help. I am looking for people who are committed, but also willing to admit they need help.

If I find deserving people, and by deserving I mean people who are ready to work, achieve, prosper and share, then I will help them. This makes me a capitalist, not a socialist. It also makes me a Leaper!

To Share is to Leverage

In the Happy Leap Year sense of sharing, we refer to the process of increasing output by using leverage; people who leverage progress geometrically, as opposed to people who do not leverage, who can only advance in a linear fashion. Let me explain.

As you know, I am a proponent of using a system of shared responsibilities and rewards. Here is how that works. When you work alone, you can only produce so much. If you work eight hours, then you get eight hours of output. However, if you team up with other people, you can multiply YOUR EFFORT THROUGH THEIR WORK.

For some people, this sounds as if you are taking advantage of other people. But remember, we are talking about building equity through a system; vastly different than working in traditional teams.

Let me be more specific. In traditional businesses, filled with employees, many companies have teams of people. Each of those teams has a leader who is responsible for the team. The leader gets paid to oversee the efforts of the team. The leader talks to the team and says, "We are all going to work together to produce something big here; if we succeed, we will all get bonuses."

Here are the problems with this system. Firstly, the leader will always get a bigger bonus than the others, even if the leader is incompetent. Secondly, some people on the team really need the bonus, so they will work harder to make sure the team gets it. Thirdly, some people on the team do not really want the bonus, or they want it but are not willing to work for it. These people work less than the people who need the money. Yet, in the end, they still get the same bonus, even though it is lower than the team leader's bonus.

In the end no one is happy, especially the company itself, because this type of team is inefficient. They split up a bonus that is well below the value that is created by the team. Most people do not give their all to this kind of system, simply because the reward structure does not promote creative, effective work and results.

But, in a *leveraged* system there are no "bonuses." Instead, everyone shares in the *profits* of the business. Sharing in the profits, with each person getting a reward commensurate with their *productivity* rather than results, means that everyone is directly tied into the profits.

Fishing Boats and Profit Sharing

To understand the concept of profit-sharing, look at the original model—fishing boats. The investors owned the boat, and hired a captain. The captain chose the crew. If the boat was successful and caught fish, everyone shared in the profits. If it lost money, no one made money.

The investors received the lion's share of the profits, because they took most of the risk. They laid out the money for the boat, the gear and the bait. The captain gets the next biggest share, then the mates, and finally the deck hands. At any time, a deck hand can work hard, learn the business, and move up to more responsibility, and a bigger share. The mates can become captains.

This is pure profit-sharing, and it works.

In the model, everyone gets a linear share of the profits. A boat can only take so many pounds of fish on board. The nets will only hold so much, and the season is limited. If they take *too* many fish on board, the boat may sink. If they fish past the end of the season, none of the legitimate fish houses will buy their catch. Even though this is profit sharing, it is still limited.

Many businesses are like this. They have some kind of limit to them. There are only so many hours in the day, and the company can only do so much business. This limit means that no one achieves geometrically; they are all limited to a linear progression. For example, the best captain in the world can only bring in as much fish as the net will hold each time. The best waiter can only serve so many tables. In fact, almost every business, and all jobs, are limited by some sort of physical or mental boundary.

You are going to overcome that by leaping into a leveraged situation. You can progress without limit, and make as much as you need. This is a giant change in thinking. You are not bound by what someone will give you, but you are also not bound by what *time and space* will permit.

Leveraging the Fishing Boats

Let's go back to the fishing boat story. Everyone who is on one boat is limited as to how much they can make, because there are limits on the boat. When a captain signs on with a boat, he is only able to work that one boat. He cannot jump from ship to ship, giving orders to two different crews. But, what if that captain saved up his money and bought a boat? Now, he gets the captain's share, and the investor's share. And, what if he makes some money and buys a second boat, and hires a captain to run the second boat. Now, he is working with leverage. He is taking his money, and putting it to work for himself. Instead of working for money, his money is working for him. This is called leverage. He is *doubling* the amount of money he can make, but not doubling his efforts.

Now, suppose the same captain buys two more boats. He is still only working on one boat, but he is getting the proceeds from four boats. As long as he hires good captains to run the other boats, he is going to make more money.

Unfortunately, most people do not think in terms of leverage. They want to trade time for dollars. This is potentially very bad because there are only so many hours in the day. Even well-paid professionals have a limit. If they charge $500 per hour, that is good money; if they work (and bill) 40 hours, they make $20,000 that week, or about $1 million per year.

What if they have a bad cold, and cannot work? In that case, the money stops. They are still tied to a "work hours for money" principle.

On the other hand, those professionals could train other people to do some of the work. Lawyers do this routinely. They train associates and secretaries to do some of the work. They can't bill as high, but they still raise healthy salaries. For example, if an attorney gets $500/hour, and her assistant gets only $100, she can still manage a team of associates, each of whom can bill at $100/hour. What if she has six associates? Now, she can do nothing but manage the associates, and still make an extra $100/hour more than if she did all the work herself.

Forget Fishing Boats and Lawyers.

"Okay" you are saying, "that is great for fishing boats and attorneys, but what about someone like me. How do I leverage my time and money?"

Let us remember that this is a book about turning Common Years into Leap Years, and about ordinary men and women making a giant Leap into a great future. We are talking about changing the present reality into one that accommodates your dreams. Of course we have a plan for ordinary men and women. This book is written by an ordinary man for people like you.

There are men and women out there who have break-through thinking and, if you take the time to listen, you will find them. When you do, you can use their example to change your life. This is how the non-lawyers, non-fishing captains, can Leap.

A few days ago, I was working on this chapter when I got a call from a radio talk show host in Jacksonville, Florida named *Richard Cuff*. Richard and I were talking about the book, and the process of establishing equity through leverage. I mentioned "Network Equity" and Richard said some things that really floored me. "I don't agree with Networking," he said. "If you really want to add value to your time, you need to form *alliances*, not networks."

Here is what he told me;

"Building a network is like collecting little bits of wire and some nuts and bolts. Nothing is finished. It is all just small parts. Maybe, after a long time of collecting these little pieces, and storing them in a drawer, you are able to sort them out and make something useful like a toaster. It takes a long time to make that toaster, and sometimes you think you are all done and you discover that there are some parts missing.

However, when you build an alliance, you start off with a toaster. In other words, you go out and find someone who has a toaster and invite them to be part of your alliance. You don't put that toaster into a drawer, you put it on a shelf where you can see it all the time, and then you go out and find some other people who have useful items. Maybe you find a frying pan, a stove, some plates and dishes, etc. Now, instead of having just a toaster (after spending all that time and effort as a networker) you have everything you need to make a meal! And, everyone gets to enjoy the meal. The person who brought the toaster gets more than just toast; the person who brought the frying pan gets more than just fried eggs; everyone is better off."

I have to tell you, I thought this was brilliant of Richard. I had never heard it before. But that is not the point. Yes, it is a great example of a powerful story, but what Richard gave me was a larger gift than a good story. He showed me the power of an alliance.

You see, I was working on *this* chapter when I spoke to Richard. (I didn't know him. He found my name on the Internet after his daughter spilled a bag of used books that she had purchased at the local library. When the books spilled to the floor, one of my books was on top of the pile. Richard picked it up and started reading it. He contacted me within the hour.)

What does all this mean? Why is it in a chapter about Watermelons and Grapes? What does it have to do with ordinary men and women?

Neither Richard nor I are famous people. But we both have businesses, and we both like to make money by sharing. Richard contacted me originally to see if I would do a recurring segment on his radio talk show. I took some time out of my schedule to speak with him because he seemed to be interesting. I got a great story for my book. I learned a cool idea about alliances versus networking. Richard gets a recurring guest on his show, and he can sell advertising on my segment.

The world is full of these opportunities. All you have to do is to *start* thinking differently. You don't have to be a professional; you just have to be open to possibilities. When people talk to you, LISTEN. You never know where the next great idea is going to come from.

What about the Grapes and Watermelons?

The title of this chapter is, "Would you rather own half a watermelon, or a whole grape?" Are you wondering what all this has to do with fruit?

I know that you can see what I mean by this title. In today's world, the way to make money is to create groups of sharing people. You need to work with others because, if you can harness their energy and potential, you can experience exponential growth. By harnessing human energy, you can unleash the power of networking and your system. Even better, you can form ALLIANCES.

Look folks, this isn't magical or mysterious; it simply works. You need to find people who want something big, and show them how to get it. If you are a Leaper, if you have decided that you will never have a common year again, then you are just the kind of person who can help other people succeed.

Make no mistake, this will only work if you help other people get what they want. This is how you build a business, and this is how you get rewards.

Yes, you can control everything, and have an entire grape. It will be small and fragile. You will be alone and will depend on your own work for rewards. If you have a whole grape, you cannot do much with it. It is nice and tidy, but it will never satisfy you.

If you have half a watermelon, it is going to be messy. If you have a half, it means that someone else has the other half.

Folks, learn to share again, but share with people who are looking for a Leap. Find them, help to train them, help them get what they want, and you can get what you want.

You may only get half a watermelon, but it is always bigger than the person who got a whole grape.

And if you don't like fruit, think about the fishing boats. Create alliances and develop profit sharing and you can reach your dreams.

In the coming Leap Year, you need to assemble a team of motivated, cheerful Leapers. In the space below, describe the type of person you are looking for. Then, describe what you will bring to the alliance. How will this help you—and them—get what each of you wants?

Resolve to share again. Resolve to share until you receive.

Chapter Ten

Can The Common Man Create An Uncommon Year?

"Aggressive play is a vital asset of the world's greatest golfers. However, it is even more important to the average player. Attack this game in a bold, confident and determined way, and you'll make a giant leap toward realizing your full potential as a player."

Greg Norman, Professional Golfer

*T*he great Australian golfer Greg Norman is known as "the Shark" because of his relentless pursuit of his goals. He has mastered the game of golf and is an excellent teacher to new professional golfers. I love his quote above, because it is so appropriate for us, the common men and women of the world.

Please read his quote carefully one more time right now. Can you see the lessons he is offering us? He knows that ordinary men and women need extraordinary effort, extraordinary thoughts and extraordinary systems if they are going to succeed.

If you are going to succeed in the new Leap Year, you need to play the game aggressively. This does not mean that you need to be ruthless. We have already determined that the great Leapers are genuinely generous. They give of themselves so that others can succeed.

However, in all games, there are certain constants, certain rules that you must follow. One of them is to throw yourself into the game, and get serious. Greg Norman calls it "bold, confident and determined."

Are You An Average Player Or A Great Professional?

The reason that I included the quote from Greg Norman is that he points out how important it is for the average person, the average player, to be bold and confident. This is such valuable information. When we watch sporting events, we cheer on the players who throw caution to the wind, and go all-out to win the game.

Yet, as Greg points out, this attitude is more important to average players. If they would just change their attitude and raise their bold confidence levels, the average player would make a much better golfer.

The same is true in becoming a great Leaper and enjoying a wonderful Happy Leap Year. In our world, we have some great professionals, and we have an enormous number of average players. In the business world, where you are building a personal, leveraged-equity, business in an effort to have an uncommon year, you must be bold, aggressive, confident and energetic—every day.

Who Are The Great Professionals?

When you first decide to become a Leaper, and to look at the world differently, you undoubtedly noticed some people who are already at the top of their business game. These are the great leaders who have already learned to leverage their time, build their businesses and place a high value on everything they do. They are bold, confident and energetic.

When we look at them, it is tempting to say, "Well sure, they can act like that. I would be bold and energetic too if I had all their money and was so successful." But, we tend to forget that they started out just like us. In the business world of wealth-seeking Leapers, everyone starts out in an equal position. In fact, no one has an advantage.

But, we look at the leaders and Leapers of today, and we forget that they started out with absolutely nothing. We don't see the home movies of Greg Norman learning to play golf like a pro and we don't see the home movies of the great personal business leaders as they tried to get their first customer.

All the fears and hassles of starting a business were there for the great leaders. They struggled. They heard "no" more times than most of us will ever hear it.

The Paradox of Power

I play a little golf. I am not very good at it, but I do like getting out on the course with some friends, wearing colors and styles that I would never wear in a civilized environment (just kidding, golfers!) There is a big difference between the way I play and the way great professionals play. Sure, they have more confidence, but they also have a different *style* of play. They are out there, every day, to win the game. I am out there to play the game. This is a huge difference.

But, here is the question. Are they confident because they are great golfers, or are they great golfers because they are confident? Did they become bold *after* they won their first championships, or are they champions because they play boldly? This is the great Paradox of Power.

Folks, I don't think there is any doubt about it. The great golfers hit the ground running. They loved the game from the time they first picked up a club, and they attacked the course each time they played. They did it to win.

Now, I think this is an interesting point. These players *loved* the game, but they never treated it as just recreation. They never thought "I will try this for another year to see if I really like it, and then if I do, I will work harder at it." Can you say the same thing about your pursuit of your dreams? Are you a professional who is out to win because there is no other way to play the game?

How many people design their dreams, and then think, "Well, I will get interested in this after I have some success?" Would you do that with your job or your profession? Would you go to a dentist who says, "I am not sure about this? I will try it and if I can stand your screaming, I will do this for a living." Or would you rather have the dentist who is calm and confident? You know the answer. But it is stunning how many people spend a lifetime at their chosen profession or career, then try to treat the pursuit of their dreams as if it was some sort of recreation, or as if they were just "trying it out."

I Hear It All the Time

I can't tell you the number of people, in all sorts of businesses, who think there is something special about the great professionals. They think the great ones are different than the average person. Even people who are extremely successful at their jobs use this as an excuse. They look at successful people and think that there is a difference between the successful people and themselves. I meet a lot of successful people in my travels, and one thing I discovered is that the vast majority of them are really ordinary people who just did the extraordinary things to succeed. The great ones are simply people with a dream, who never quit no matter what happens.

And, a lot happened to them! They all have great stories. If you listen to them carefully, they all say the same things. "I decided to change my life because _____ (Problem Recognition). I wanted this ___ (Dream) but, when I first started out, some bad things happened and I almost quit. What kept me going was my dream. I wanted it so bad. I knew I had to change in order to be successful, because my attitude of _____ (negative behavior or belief) was holding me back. I soon realized that if I could just do _____ (work the system) enough times, I would have all the things I wanted. Luckily, I met _____ (an ordinary person who, by that time, had become a great Leaper) and she/he was so generous with their help; soon, I was succeeding."

That is the success story of almost everyone I know. They found some kind of reason to build wealth-generating networks and alliances. It was some kind of Problem Recognition, coupled with their desire to achieve their dream.

None of them started out well. Almost all of them had setbacks. But, they wanted what they wanted; they had a dream and they would not be denied.

Most of them met someone who was already successful in their business. They followed the advice of the Leapers they met, and used their mentors' system to keep going.

By the time I met them, they were great professionals, playing aggressively, confidently and energetically. But, they *learned* to do that, and they were not successful until they learned it.

Are You A Leaper In A Common Body?

Who are the common men and women who will become great players? There is no way to tell by looking at them when they are new Leapers. They could be anybody. I can't tell you who they are, and you don't even know if *you* will be one of the great ones.

Why is that? Aren't there some traits that make some people better than others? Can't we administer a test to see who will be a winner, and who will not?

We cannot do this, for a very special reason. There are no hereditary traits that make people great. They are all learned, and they can be learned at any time. The reason we cannot tell who will be great is because even the most ordinary person can change and become great, if something happens to them. What is that "something?" All the great players are pursuing their dreams with excitement and enthusiasm. Something happened to them that helped to trigger their need to reach their dreams. Then, they *learned* what to do to achieve the dream.

This is why I think that postponing your quest while you *gather more information* is such a bad idea. It isn't the *information* that will make you successful; the things that make a person successful all come from our personal qualities, and each of us has complete control over these qualities.

Isn't that an interesting thought? It isn't the *business*; it is the *business men and women* that determine success.

All you have to do is to look at what successful people are doing, and do that as well—again and again. You don't need to reinvent the wheel. You just need to get on a wheel and ride it along with the other Leapers who have figured it out.

First Half, Second Half, Overtime, or Sudden Death?

What part of the game are you playing? Are you in the first half, the second half, overtime or sudden death? It all depends on your dream and your current situation. If you are still young, and have a secure job, you may be in the first half of the game. You may not be in such a hurry. You think you have time. On the other hand, if you are older, with some expenses looming, you may be in the second half. You definitely have less time. You need to step up your aggressive playing.

If you are in Overtime, it is either because you are older, or because you have some specific, urgent need for success. Overtime players have no choice. They need to be aggressive to win. They need to overcome their fears IMMEDIATELY and get to work. They can't use excuses. They need results fast, and that means that they are going to have to skip the "learning curve," and start doing what successful people do immediately.

Of course, if this is really your last chance, if you are in trouble because you are much older, or because your job has ended, or because your industry is falling apart and you have bills to pay, you have NO time for fooling around. You have to go right from the Caddy Shack to the clubhouse!

The way you change, the way you work, is completely dependent on where you are in the game. For me, at 58, I am definitely late in the second half. I don't have time to waste on people or practices that just don't seem to be working. I am ready to work with ANYONE who is on the move, but I will not be held back by those who can't make the right changes and who cannot act like a professional who is "in it to win it."

In fact, I am getting ready to play in overtime, and then the play will get even more serious. I know who I am and where I am, and I am planning to act accordingly.

As Greg Norman says, "The common man must play confidently, boldly and energetically." I say this is true, and the common man who is in the second half or later must do it now.

Are you In It to Win It?

Success requires personal growth. If it didn't, you would already be successful. Just changing careers, or creating a new business, will not make you successful… It will not help you reach your dreams.

To be successful, you need to do five things (Is this sounding familiar?) Realize you have a problem, get a dream, commit to the dream, find successful people who have already solved your problem and execute a plan as often as needed.

Determine your need for speed by looking at the problems you face. If you don't really need more money, more time and more *lifestyle*, then you can take your time. If you are in NEED, then act like it and do what you NEED to do!

Finally, if you are not the man or woman you need to be, change, and become the man or woman you CAN be. If you do, you will make a great Leap, and have a Happy Leap Year.

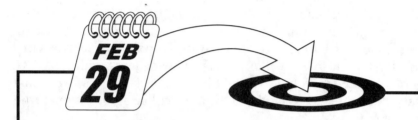

To be successful, you need to be bold, energetic and confident. In the space below, describe what your income, health and relationships would be like if you were to start playing the game of life boldly, energetically, and confidently.

Resolve to become those things, starting now! (Notice that none of these three traits is "outcome based." They are behavioral, which means you can start acting like that right now. RESOLVE!

Chapter Eleven

Why Doesn't Everyone Have A Happy Leap Year?

"Many people look forward to the New Year for a new start on old habits."

Anonymous

*A*fter reading the first 10 chapters of this book, you might be asking yourself the question that is the title of this chapter. "Why Doesn't Everyone Have A Happy Leap Year?" After all, isn't it relatively simple to take a great Leap in the New Year, and can't anyone start their Leap Year at any time?

There are really two reasons why people do not have Happy Leap Years. The first factor, Fear, holds them back. The second factor, Greed, kills their businesses after they have grown, and are building equity with alliances and networks. In this chapter, we are going to look at the paralyzing effects of Fear—how it is the biggest killer of Leap Years, and we will show how the vice of Greed can kill and ruin profitable relationships. If you can learn to overcome Fear, and avoid Greed, you can have the Happiest of Happy Leap Years—starting right now!

Interestingly, both Fear and Greed are particularly unattractive human faults. I find them both offensive, because they are spirit-killers. People who are afraid cannot fulfill their destinies; their fear is contagious, and it infects others. (Usually it infects the people I am trying to work with, so it REALLY upsets me!) Greed is a spirit-killer because it takes away from others. The greedy person is on a mission to gather up all the rewards, and keep them for him/herself.

In this chapter we are going to discuss how to avoid these two ugly siblings. You will learn how to banish them from your own life, and also how to avoid people who suffer from them .

Meet Sibling #1 – Fear

There are times when fear is a useful emotion. When cavemen roamed the earth, and any trip to the local stream could involve a meeting with a saber-toothed tiger, a little fear was just the emotion needed to keep people alive. Even today, when confronted with physical danger, experiencing fear might save your life. Fear produces a "Flight or Fight" reaction in humans. With the adrenalin pumping, you have to make a split-second decision whether to face the situation, confront the cause of the fear or run for the hills. There are times when each decision could be right.

When I first left college, I joined an organization called "VISTA." It was like the Peace Corps but, instead of traveling to foreign lands, we worked right here in the United States. Because of my background, I found myself assigned to a terribly dangerous neighborhood in Cleveland, Ohio, called The Hugh. I worked with minority-owned businesses there.

One of my jobs was to take the money from two fast food restaurants to the bank each night. Now, you have to understand the situation. I am white, and no one else in that neighborhood was white. I stuck out. In fact, some of the people referred to me as the "light bulb." Not only was I highly visible because of the color of my skin, I was also easy to spot as two policemen escorted me to the bank with the cash each night!

Why am I telling you this? I want you to know that I understand real Fear. I know just how much it makes your knees weak and your stomach hurt. I understand the "flight or fight" question, and I want to tell you that I used "flight" on many occasions during my one-year service tour (I was not eligible for the Armed Services because of my eyesight, and I wanted to serve my country and my fellow man in some way.) If I had known **EXACTLY** what I would be doing, and how often I would have been attacked and chased, I would have thought of a better way!

So, Fear can be helpful. If you channel it into positive action, it is even exhilarating in a way. It kept me focused, I can tell you that. In fact, the only time I was successfully robbed was when I had let my guard down and was not paying attention to my surroundings. Four young men caught me and took my money. (Ironically, I was on the way home from Karate Class!)

But folks, while Fear is good in extreme circumstances, it is very, very bad when it comes to something less extreme like deciding that it's time to shout "Happy Leap Year." Unfortunately, people allow their fears of minor things, or worse, IMAGINED things, to keep them from enjoying all the benefits of life.

What Are You Afraid Of?

It is amazing what people are afraid of, and what they are NOT afraid of. Every day, millions of people get up and go to work at a job they don't really like, or, at least, at a job where they are under-valued. Yet, are they afraid that this is how they are going to spend the rest of their lives? No, that isn't what they are afraid of; they ACCEPT that this is the way things are going to be.

Yet, these same people are so afraid to change their lives for the better by taking a Leap out of the maze that has kept them in debt all their lives. Why are they afraid? Is it because they are afraid of losing their money? No, it is often because their neighbors might think they are a little crazy! How is this possible? How can a rational human being be afraid of what other people think? Will those other people pay your bills? Will they support you when you get laid off? Will they pay for your kids' tuition?

As I travel around the world, speaking to groups, I hear the same thing again and again; "I am afraid my boss will fire me" or, "I don't want to lose my reputation." I can understand that you do not want any of these things to happen to you. No one wants to be fired, or have a bad reputation. But what I don't understand is why these fears are bigger than the ones you SHOULD have. Why aren't the really big fears like "I will waste an entire lifetime that could have been better" or "If I don't show my kids how to overcome any adversity and reach their dreams, who will?" Now, those are fears worth having. Being afraid to be different—especially if being different is better than being average—is not a good fear.

What about My Boss?

From reading this book, you know that I advise people to Leap into new ways of thinking, and to build an equity-driven source of recurring income (while maintaining your primary source of income, such as your job.) I understand that people have concerns about getting fired because their boss finds out that they are building equity. You want to protect that source of income, but you also want to protect your family's future.

Let me throw out a few thoughts on the whole "I can't build equity because my boss might fire me" fear.

- Never conduct personal business on company time, or with company assets, or on company property. Not only is that dangerous, it is unethical

- Does your boss own your time 24/7/366? If he/she does, you need to change jobs anyway. What you do on your own time is your own business (pun intended)

- Don't give your boss a reason to complain. Be the very best employee on the job. In fact, by learning to Leap, Leverage and Build Equity, you are bound to become better, because you will understand how business works

- Are you worried about your boss using your excitement and enthusiasm for building financial security as an excuse to lay you off? Don't worry about that; chances are good that you were going to get laid-off anyway. If you have a recurring income generated by equity, you have someplace to go!

Folks, here is the basic truth about being afraid of losing your job because you are creating security for your family. It is an excuse, as are most fears.

I also mentioned that people are afraid of their reputations being ruined because they choose to act differently. Here are some common excuses (I mean "expressions of fear") that I hear from people who are afraid of damaging their reputations.

- **"If I tell my friends about this, they will think I am crazy."** Well, your good friends already think you are little nuts, but they still like you. But even if they don't, does it really matter, when your future, and the future of your children, are at stake?

- **"My relatives will think I am crazy."** If you have relatives like mine, *they* are already a little crazy. Is this really a concern?

- **"I am a physician (engineer, lawyer, etc.). People will think that my business isn't going well."** Here is something you need to know. People are not thinking about you. They are thinking about themselves

Here is what I know about reputations—they don't rise and fall because you decided to create personal wealth. They rise and fall because you are either an ethical person or you are not. If you are ethical, honest, kind and friendly, do you really think that your reputation depends on you doing the same thing everyone else is doing. Wouldn't you *rather* have a reputation as a spirited, adventurous LEAPER? Again, worrying about your reputation is an excuse.

Finally, here is a third category of fears - the fear of failure. I hear people say some very strange things in this category. Actually, you will probably be surprised at what I *put* into this category of fears.

- **"This will cost me a lot of time and money."** This is simply not true. I am not advising you to make huge investments of time and money. In fact, I am showing you how to *reduce* your inputs, and increase your outputs. Right now, how much money do you waste by under-valuing yourself. As for time—what are you doing with yours right now? Couldn't you shift a few hours away from the television and watch your future, instead of watching reruns of a sitcom?

- **"I am not good at organizing myself, building customers, public speaking, accounting, etc."** (These are some of the things that Leapers do to leverage their time and money.) No, you are just afraid to build a business. No one is good at that stuff—at first

- **"I don't have enough information. Maybe I should study this for a while, and then I will feel comfortable making a Leap."** No one ever has ALL the information they need. It would be impossible. This is a very common excuse, and is just a cover-up for fear of failure

I believe most of these things are just a set of excuses to cover up the fact that you are afraid. I would love to hear someone say, "Well, I would change my life and become a Leaper, but I have all these fears. I am afraid." At least that would be honest. Instead, I hear people use all these great excuses. They don't want to say, "I am afraid" so they come up with something that sounds reasonable. Most of the people who express their fear through excuses really believe that the excuses are valid.

Overcoming Fear

The first step towards overcoming fear in others is to overcome it in yourself. We are all afraid, and that is the first thing to admit. In order to overcome fear about our bosses, our reputations, our failures etc., we must create another fear that is so strong that we become more afraid of the second fear, and forget about the first. Or, even if we don't *forget* about our boss/reputation/failure fears, we are willing to work through them because the other fear is just too strong.

What should we fear more than our fears? How about, "Not ever reaching my dreams?" Remember, I told you that you have to develop a dream and then commit to it. If you develop a strong enough dream, and if you make it so real that you cannot imagine not having it, then the fear of losing that dream will be enough to overcome your fears about the other stuff.

When Jeanne and I decided, on that day in 1993, that we would find a way to live on the water, we did everything we could to make that dream as real as possible. We cut out pictures of boats and put them on the refrigerator. We cut out pictures of houses. We *talked* about our dreams constantly. We wrote them down and looked at them every day. The pain of not having those things was so strong that I was able to overcome my fears and achieve my dreams.

Folks, I just don't know any other way to do it. Everyone is afraid, so you can't just tell them not to be. If you are serious about achieving your dreams, and if your dreams are strong enough and worthwhile enough, you can achieve almost anything—despite your fears. You can even inspire others to do the same.

Success Overcomes Fear

Success is a great motivator. However, you may not have a history of success. Most of us do not. When I first decided to start writing books for money, my first FIVE books were commercial failures. Can you imagine that? Would you have kept writing books? It was tough.

But, I began to watch other authors, and to do what they did. I learned to change because I wanted to achieve my dreams. I did whatever it takes—literally, and my sixth book was a success. In fact, it was a best-seller.

Was it *my own success* that inspired me while my first five books were failing? No, it was the success of some people who I admired, and who showed me what they were doing in order to give me hope. I kept going because of their successes, not mine. But, I also knew that those people were no better than me. I got to know them and it was easy to see that they were good, but not perfect.

So, here are two secrets for you. First, make your dreams real and make the pain of losing them bigger than the pain of the work. In addition, try to meet successful people and learn more about them. You will see that they do not have any more talent than you do. They are just able to overcome their fears better. They have a dream that is so strong that they can forge ahead, even when they are afraid.

Just Do This One Thing

Jeanne and I set one goal for ourselves that really helped us achieve our dreams—despite our fears. We said, "We will not let the sun set on a day when we did not take at least one step towards achieving our dreams." This simple statement really helped. Every day, we did something. It may have been reading a positive book (like this one.) Or, it might have been some more complicated work. It didn't matter what it was, we just did it every day. At first, it was little things that really didn't take giant Leaps forward. But, after a while, we got bolder and did the big things that helped us move to the water, and put a big boat in the backyard.

And, What about Greed?

In the beginning of this chapter, I talked about the two siblings, Fear and Greed. So, what about Greed? Greed doesn't stop you from *starting* your journey towards success and security; it *destroys* it after you build alliances, networks and income. Despite Michael Douglas' proclamation as Gordon Gekko, in the original version of the movie *Wall Street* that "Greed is good," I can promise you that greedy people fail to Leap and Leverage their way to security and true success.

In the chapter, "Would You Rather Own Half a Watermelon than a Whole Grape?" we say that greedy people can own a whole grape, but they will never get people to cooperate with them to create a half-watermelon sized business. The best way to reduce inputs and increase outputs is to create teams of people who *share in the profits*. Everyone who produces results gets a share commensurate with their achievement. If you start taking more than your fair share, you will lose the faith of the people you are building your equity with.

Greedy People Do Not Have Leverage

One of the quickest and surest ways to achieve success is to build leverage. The only way you can do this is to build a team of people who are willing to continue working with you. As they become more successful, you become more successful—but only if they keep doing it! Another HUGE advantage of leverage is that, when you stop working, the money keeps rolling in because other people are working. Again, this only works if those other people have an incentive to keep working.

In fact, becoming *generous* (the opposite of being *greedy*) is so fundamentally important to building your personal success that you must learn to practice it every day, with every person you meet.

By the way, despite the rumors to the contrary, being generous does not cost you anything. In fact, it makes you a lot of money. But, because we are trained to think that generosity is almost always money-based, most people assume they will have to pay for their generous spirit.

Here is a great anti-greed secret. I have made a lot of money because people come to me with their ideas. They know that I am always looking for new, money-making ventures. Most of the ideas that I hear are not that good, but I listen to all of them anyway. However, every now and then, a really spectacular one comes along. When it does, I either try to work in an alliance myself, or I introduce the person with the idea to some of my partners who can help him/her.

Does listening to ideas cost me money? No: does it cost me time? Yes: a little, but I have worked out ways to reduce the time I need to spend on each idea.

On the other hand, when you get a reputation for listening to others, you also gain a reputation for being generous with your time. Being "generous" is actually a selfish act, because it is a fantastic way to Leverage. For example, I can't possibly come up with a list of great ideas each time I want to write a book or create a new income stream. If people know that they can bring me ideas, and that I will share rewards with them, then *they* are doing idea-generating work for me! Can you see how this Leverages my time, instead of costing me time?

The same theory applies to working with other people in networks or alliances. I make sure that I give them what they want and need for their personal success. If I do that enough times, I get a reputation for generosity, and people do things for me in return. Again, this is a Leveraging technique.

Being generous is the opposite of being greedy. Being generous is also the foundation for making more money, having more time, and getting more rewards. Learn to overcome your greed, and you will be surprised at how your wealth grows.

Of course, if you give to people and they only take from you— with no returns—you have just identified a greedy person. Stay away from them; greedy people will kill you with their greed.

When you think about other greedy people, and how you feel about them, you begin to realize just how damaging it is to be thought of as greedy. Observe the Golden Rule—"Do unto others as you would have them do unto you." Then, enjoy the Leverage.

Do You Want A Happy Leap Year?

If you want to take a giant Leap, and if you want to be one of the "lucky ones" (as if "luck" has anything to do with it,) you now know two things. First, build a big dream and commit to it so that the pain of not having your dream is worse than the pain from your fears. Second, do not succumb to temptation as you start to build your wealth. Be generous, not greedy, and help everyone else get what they want. You will find that you will get what you want—and still have friends to share the excitement with.

In previous "Resolutions" we have already talked about some of your fears. Now, it is time to face up to your greed! In the space below, describe a greedy person you know and how it makes you feel to be around that person. Next, carefully list the things you do that could mark you as a greedy person.

Resolve to overcome your greed. Resolve to be generous.

Chapter Twelve

Where Will You Be in a Leap Year?

"This is one small step for man and one giant leap for mankind."

Neil Armstrong
Astronaut and first man to walk on the moon

Whenever the traditional New Year's Celebration rolls around, people often ask themselves, "Where will we be in a year?" I am asking you a slightly different question. "Where will you be in a Leap Year?" But, I have a second question for you. "Where will you be if you do not make this year a Leap Year?"

Remember, you now know that there are two kinds of years—common years and Leap Years. A common year has all the old rules and traditions. A Leap Year not only gives you an extra day, it also gives you the excuse to think and act differently. Will you take the opportunity to declare this a Leap Year? Will you be daring, resourceful, bold and energetic? Will you create wealth in yourself by creating wealth in others, and display your generous spirit? Or, will you spend the next year doing the exact same things you did every year before - trading your time for dollars and working for someone else's dream?

In this chapter, the final chapter, we will look at the two paths you might take in the coming year. Then, you must answer the question, "Will this be a common year, or a Leap Year, and where will I be at the end of it?"

Will You Be Ready For Inspiration?

I told you already about the day my life changed, and I made my first Leap. It was July 7, 1993, at 2:30 in the afternoon. When that large yacht passed our dockside table, I was ready to receive inspiration because I already had Problem Recognition, and I already had a dream.

Today, November 28, 2010, I received some more inspiration. I was in church with my family, when Pastor Brian Roberts gave a sermon on changing our attitudes. In fact, he specifically asked the question, "What will happen in the next year?" He then delivered the messages that are the framework for this chapter.

Now, let's think about this. I was in church, listening to the sermon, but because I had opened my mind to new thoughts, I received the inspiration for the final chapter—often the most difficult to write. I was writing a book about Leap Year, and the pastor delivered the message I needed to hear.

If I hadn't prepared myself, if I wasn't already *thinking* about what I needed to do, I would have listened to his sermon and thought, "Well, that was nice," and gone about my business, without making a significant change or accomplishing a major goal.

What about you? Are you ready to open your mind, and invite inspiration into your heart? Are you prepared to make this a Leap Year, with all the changes, growth and accomplishments that it could bring you? You see, folks, you have to be ready 24/7/366! Once you dedicate your life to making your dreams come true, you must remain attentive, alert and prepared to absorb any message that will help you in your cause.

When I ask you, "Where will you be in a Leap Year?", your answer will depend entirely on how well you are prepared.

So, with great thanks to Pastor Brian Roberts, let's finish this chapter, and this book. I provided you with the information you need to get started. The rest is up to you. Will you be prepared to act, to think, and to LEAP?

The Things We Think We Don't Know

We assume that we do not know a lot of things. For example, if I asked you, "Where will the stock market be in a year?", you would probably tell me you do not know. If I asked, "What will the world be like in a year?", you would probably tell me that you do not know exactly. If I said to you, "How much will you be making on your job in a year?", you might also have problems answering that question, because of the uncertainty with companies today.

Now, let's look at this in a different light. You certainly can't tell me with *absolute certainty* the New York Stock Exchange's value in 366 days, but you know that it will be *something*. You don't know *exactly* what the world will look like, but you know that the Middle East will be experiencing unrest, China will be lending us money and trying to take over the top economic position in the world, the U.S. Congress will have talked a lot, but done very little, and there will be earthquakes and other natural disasters somewhere in the world.

On your job, your boss will have good days and bad days (which will make your days good or bad) and there will be talk about cutting back and saving money. (I was a college professor for twenty-five years, and we talked about cutbacks and budgets at EVERY, SINGLE meeting for twenty-five years. In fact, I am positive they are still talking about it!)

In other words, folks, we think that we do not know a lot of things. We say things like, "How should I know what to do? I am not a fortune teller! I can't say what is going to happen." But, that just isn't true. We do know what is going to happen. We know because it has always happened. All we have to do to understand the future is to look at the past and the present. The past and the present *are* the future.

Today, Pastor Brian read from the Old Testament. I forget which passage it was, but it talked about political unrest, a poor economy, bad behavior and fear of attacks. How many thousands of years ago was that? Yet, the same conditions persist today.

The truth is, you know a lot of things, and if you don't start acting like you know what has happened before, you will always be at the mercy of what is about to happen.

While you may not have control over the events around you, you have perfect control over the attitudes, beliefs and actions that are inside you. You can be the master of your own personality and outcomes. You know you can, because in reality, you know **EXACTLY** what is going to happen in the coming year.

What Will You Have For Dinner In 366 Days?

Brian Roberts made a hilarious observation today. He said, "My wife could tell you what I would order from a menu a year from now. I could tell you which story my friend will be telling at a party a year from now. The reason we know these things is because we know ourselves, and we know others. My wife knows what I like to eat; I know what my friends will talk about."

Are you beginning to understand why I was so excited about the sermon today? We pretend we don't know what is going to happen, but we are just kidding ourselves. We do know what is going to happen. We know what our friends will do, what our spouses will do, and what we will do. If you order the steak at a restaurant because you do not like to eat fish, you are not going to change in a year, unless you make a *decision* to change—for some reason—and then act on that decision. If you are overweight now, you will be overweight a year from now unless you make a decision to change, then act on that decision consistently. If you are in financial difficulty today, or facing uncertainty, or afraid, or *whatever*, you will be exactly the same a year from now—unless you make a decision and make it a Happy Leap Year for the next 366 days.

Folks, you are looking at a year of your life coming up. What will you do? What will you decide? Will you be doing the same things a year from now, or will you have made significant changes and ended up in a new place, with new accomplishments?

Your Common Year Outcomes

Okay, let's look at the outcomes of your upcoming year if it is a common year. You know what a common year is; it is any year that is not a Leap Year. It has 365 days, and you will spend your time just like you always have.

To examine the upcoming common year, just look at the past years. But, do it in light of the information from this book.

One of the most important questions I asked you in this book was, "Do you own your life, or are you just renting?" In that chapter, I pointed out the dangers of trading your time for dollars, buying things on credit, and looking for raises to finance your life. If you do all these things, you are a virtual slave to anyone who will hire you, and your life will be permanently under-valued. You will pass along these lessons to your children, and they will be virtual slaves as well. If you want to own your life, you must create equity, and then let the equity make money for you so that you have the time to enjoy it.

If the upcoming year is a common year, is there any reason to believe that things will be different than they are now? I don't think so. In a common year, what are you doing to create equity? Have you invested in building alliances and a network of people who are all striving to achieve their dreams? The truth is, at the end of the next common year, you will still be a slave to another person. At the end of the next common year, you will be in the same position AT BEST, and in even more trouble at worst. There is no positive upside here.

Your upcoming common year is just one in a long string of common years—if you are lucky enough to have a long string of them! It is like staying in that maze, looking ahead to the next obstacle, trying to find a way out.

For 99% of the people in the world, the next year will be a common year, because they did not find the spark, the inspiration, that one thing that gives them a sense of Problem Recognition. And sadly, for at least 50% of the people reading this book, the next year will be a common year because you either didn't have Problem Recognition, or you did, and ignored it.

For the vast majority of people, the next year will be a common year filled with common fears. These fears will be masked by excuses, but no matter, the result is the same whether it is a fear or a fear-caused excuse. It means postponing, maybe even eliminating, the achievement of a worthwhile dream.

Another common year is a dismal prospect, isn't it? How many more common years do you have? How long will you wait before you say, "Enough is enough," and make some serious changes? How long will it be before you Leap into a New Year? Will it ever happen?

Your Uncommon (Leap) Year Outcomes

Where will you be in a year if you embrace the strategies and philosophies of a Leaper? Interestingly, this is less certain than the outcomes for a common year. We know how the common year will end up because we can look back at all the common years we spent. But a Leap Year is an uncommon year. For this reason, we cannot accurately predict the future of a Leap Year.

This is one of the big reasons people never try to Leap. They don't have the certainty of mediocrity that they have with a common year. They know they will be mediocre in a common year, but they can't be sure they will achieve anything by working in a Leap Year. So this uncertainty turns into fear, and this fear turns into excuses, and the excuses turn into—nothing!

But I hope, after reading this book, you now understand that you are making a choice every time you learn something. In this book, you learned about the beauty of building a strong dream, then doing everything in your power to achieve it. You learned how to leap over obstacles. If you don't, you are making a conscious choice to stay where you are.

Here is one thing I *can* tell you with certainty. Even if you make only small gains this coming Leap Year, you are far better off than if you do nothing. It doesn't matter if you reach all of your dreams in a single year. What matters is that you *begin* the struggle, by building your dreams and taking a small step.

Look at the quote at the beginning of this chapter. It is the famous Neil Armstrong quote when he first stepped onto the surface of the moon; "This is one small step for man, one giant leap for mankind."

To have a successful Leap Year, and to be in a better place a year from now, you don't have to solve all your problems the first day. All you need to do to start your Leap Year is to *recognize* that you have a problem, then define your dream and commit to it.

How can you cut down the uncertainty of a Leap Year? You can do it by concentrating on achieving some small success at first, then building. Here is a small success you can start with—decide you are going to commit to a dream.

Here are some simple steps to work on during the Leap Year:

- Commit to your dream, and specifically define it
- Associate with positive, successful people
- Concentrate on equity building, but start small
- Concentrate on helping others achieve their dreams. Be a generous giver so that you will be a gracious and appreciative receiver
- Add value to other people's lives
- Accurately estimate your own value, and then build that value by creating equity and helping others
- Concentrate on being a good example - to your children and spouse first, then to the wider community
- Recognize your fears for what they are, and don't make excuses to cover up your fears. Overcome the fears by concentrating on the dreams. Make "not achieving my dreams" the biggest fear

- Follow my example, and "Never let the sun set on a day when you didn't take one step forward towards your dreams"

When you look at that bulleted list, do you see anything there that you cannot do? And, although you cannot say exactly where you will be after a year of Leaping, can you see that you will be better off than if you do the same things you always did?

Slow Is Faster Than Never

About six months ago, I was working with a newbie author who was trying to write her first book. She said to me, "I don't know how you do it. You write so quickly; I am writing so slowly. Will I ever get this book finished?" I felt sorry for her. She really wanted to get a book out. She was thinking that it was taking too long, and that she was doing something wrong.

However, sometimes inspiration hits me, and I am able to say something that really makes a difference in someone's life. In fact, this newbie author is always reminding me that I said this to her; "Slow is faster than never."

I want to share this same phrase with you, because it may make a difference to some of you. Yes, it is best to move quickly and decisively, and to reach your goals immediately, but it really doesn't matter how long it takes as long as you reach them.

When you tell your story, would you rather say, "I never reached my goals because I never even started" or, "It took me a long time to reach my goals, but we never stopped working at it. Finally, after much struggle, we did it." I don't think there is any doubt about it. You would rather tell the second story, wouldn't you? (Of course, if you can only tell the first story, you will be telling it to a bunch of people who never started as well. If you can tell the second story, you will be telling it from stages around the world, to people who are excited, proud, confident and bold.)

Folks, there is only one measure of your Leap Year success. *Did you start it?* Everything after that is just a matter of degree!

Ready, Set, START...

Every book must come to an end, and this is it! Where am I leaving you? I am leaving you at the beginning of your uncommon year, and therefore, at the start of your uncommon life. I am imagining the beginning of a great race. I am looking around the starting line, seeing all of you, ready to go, ready to race. It is a grand sight. Everyone is excited. Everyone is looking *forward*, and everyone will take off running when the starter's pistol goes off.

Take a moment, and put yourself into that scene. How are you dressed? You know what I look like. Just look at the picture of me from 1967. I am wearing that same track suit, although it is a few sizes larger, the hair is now all gray (but still there), and my face reflects the years of life that separate me from that picture.

What do the people look like around us? Do you recognize them? Are they the kind of people you want to run with?

When the gun goes off, some of us will run fast; others, not so fast. Many of us will stumble along the way. Some will get up, and some will stay down.

But, everyone in the Leap Year race is moving forward, each at our own pace and each towards our own goals. Some of us run with companions, others run alone. No matter, we will find company along the way. It is easy to make friends with people who are moving in the same direction we are.

I may not see you at the finish. That isn't important. As long as I see you at the start and as long as I see you begin the race when the gun goes off.

Enjoy the race, but enjoy it by starting!

Here we go. The starter shouts "Ready, Set, GO" The gun goes off, and the race begins.

Happy Leap Year!

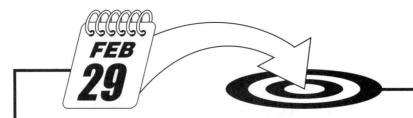

You now have all the tools you need. It is time to get started.
If you found your motivation to start the Leap Year in this book,
write down a few notes about it in the space below.
If it came from somewhere else, write something down about that.

Most importantly, however, write down the date you started,
or will start, your Happy Leap Year Journey. Resolve to fulfill your
destiny in the next 366 days. BEGIN!

About the Author

Bill Quain is the author of 19 books on Marketing, Personal Success, and Free Enterprise. He has sold more than 2 million copies, and his books are translated into 20 languages. Dr. Quain travels extensively, speaking to audiences of all sizes. Besides the United States, he has been a speaker in China, Canada, The United Kingdom, Mexico, Europe and the Carribean.

Dr. Quain was a business professor for more than 25 years. He was named "Outstanding Teaching Professor" by four universities. His students learned more than just theories, as Dr. Quain challenged them with real-life examples. Unlike most faculty members, who taught students to, "Settle for a job, and ask for raises to survive," he taught his students to create wealth through personal initiative. He wanted to give his students the keys to Financial Freedom.

He graduated from Cornell University, Florida International University and the University of New Orleans. Before entering academia, he owned and operated a hotel, was a Food and Beverage Director and an Executive Chef. For many years he has been a business consultant and analyst.

Bill Quain began to lose his eyesight to Macular Degeneration at the age of 14. Today, he is legally blind. However, he does not let his condition slow him down. In 2001 he co-created and hosted a PBS television cooking show for the blind called *Cooking Without Looking*. In 2006 Oscar-winning actress Marlee Matlin asked him to appear on ABC's *Extreme Makeover, Home Edition*. Bill cannot drive a car, but he solved his transportation problems at Florida International University in Miami by kayaking to work for six years.

Bill Quain now lives in Ocean City, New Jersey with his wife Jeanne, and two daughters. For more information about Dr. Quain, visit his website at *www.quain.com*.